MY BODY, MYSELF

Anita Naik has been a freelance journalist for the past five years. She works for teenage and women's magazines, newspapers and television, and is *Just 17*'s resident agony aunt.

The author and publisher would like to thank everyone who has contributed to this book. Many of the facts and figures come from the following sources:

'A Fresh Start' (Tampax leaflet); 'Confidentiality and People Under 16' (BMA/Brook/FPA); 'Contraception for Men' (Boots information leaflet); Daily Mail; Department of Health; Evening Standard; Family Planning Association press releases; FPA/*Just 17* Education Survey; 'Getting to Know Your Body' (Unipath leaflet); Girl About Town; Guardian; Health Education Authority; Health Education Council pamphlets; Institute for the Study of Drug Dependence; Mintel; MS Society; 'Say Yes? Say No? Say Maybe?' (Brook Advisory Pamphlet); TNT; 'Wise up to Condoms' (Durex leaflet).

My Body, Myself

THE ULTIMATE HEALTH BOOK
FOR GIRLS

Anita Naik

MACMILLAN

First published 1996 by
Macmillan Children's Books
a division of Macmillan Publishers Ltd
25 Eccleston Place, London SW1W 9NF
and Basingstoke

Associated companies throughout the world

ISBN 0 330 34333 5

Copyright © Anita Naik 1996

1 3 5 7 9 8 6 4 2

A CIP catalogue record for this book is available from the British Library.

Phototypeset by Intype London Ltd
Printed by Mackays of Chatham plc, Chatham, Kent

In memory of Louisa Nellist for putting her heart and soul into teenage issues and for saving this book at the very last minute.

Contents

Introduction

Who do you go to when you need help? A friend, a parent, a sister? Or do you hide in your room and cry because you're afraid and worried about what's happening to you and you don't know where to turn? If you do then you're not alone. Hundreds of teenagers are probably doing that or at least thinking of that right now. Growing up is a scary thing – talk to any adult and they'll say they wouldn't go through it again for a million pounds. There's no other time in your life when you'll be faced with so many choices, emotions and bodily changes all at once. And no other time when people will be so unsympathetic to these changes.

This book will help you find a way through this confusing time. In order to be in control of your body you need to be in control of your emotions and this can be hard to do when you don't know what's happening to either. If you are prepared for these changes and know what to expect from the things that may happen to your body, you are going to know how to deal with them in a practical and straightforward matter.

This means talking to someone when you're worried about a rash, a possible lump or a weird discharge. It doesn't mean crying in your room and worrying if you are weird or dying. There is a wealth of places you can go to for help. If speaking to your parents or teachers is out of the question then there are other people's parents, helplines, pharmacists at your local chemist's, and more importantly your doctor.

Doctors have the expertise and knowledge to help you and you should not be afraid of going to see them. Although this book is a health book, it isn't here to diagnose yourself with. It's here to tell you a little about what's worrying you or what might worry you, and to point you in the right direction to find out more. Don't suffer in silence.

Chapter One

HEALTH AND THE LAW

Being a teenager is hard. Being a teenager with a health problem is even harder. When you're a child, being ill is relatively easy. You get ill, you tell your parents, they call a doctor, he or she examines you, and you get better. As a teenager it's just not that easy. For a start you want a bit more privacy when it comes to being ill. You may not want your parents involved because you may feel your problem is too intimate, or perhaps you're afraid that they just won't understand what's troubling you. This leads to more problems because you may end up feeling it's easier to suffer in silence than attempt to get any help for yourself.

Then there's the problem of where to go for help. It's scary enough to find a suspicious lump or to have a strange discharge without knowing who can help you. Likewise if you want to go on the pill or need to talk to someone about a sexual problem, who can you trust not to tell your parents? The fact is, whether you realize it or not, you have rights when it comes to your body and health.

Don't be like one 15-year-old girl who was too afraid to see her GP when she discovered a lump in her breast. She automatically assumed that the lump meant cancer and became convinced that she was going to die. As a result she started skipping school, ignoring her friends and refusing to eat. She became so depressed that she just cried all the time. Finally her sister managed to find out what was happening and took her to the doctor only to discover that the 'lump' was just her breasts developing. It may sound a ridiculous story, but how many times have you lain awake at night believing you were seriously ill and yet, at the same time, were too afraid to do anything about it?

If you have then you probably don't know the answers to the following questions.

- Do you know what your rights are?
- Do you know what kind of help you are entitled to?
- Do you know what kind of health services are free to you?
- Do you know what your parents can and can't make you do?

If you're anything like the kind of teenager I was, the answer to all these questions is probably – 'No.' After all, how are you supposed to know this kind of information? None of us are told these things at school, our parents probably don't know most of them, and unless you have a particularly clued-up relative or friend you could go through your whole life knowing very little or, worse still, knowing the wrong things.

It is important to know exactly what your health rights are because it's the only way to protect yourself. And in order to stay healthy and happy you also have to know how and where to get help when you need it. This will also empower you and help you to be assertive if anyone ever tries to persuade you into something you don't want to do.

'The whole sexual thing is confusing. My friends say if you have sex and you are under 16 no one is allowed to help you without telling your parents. Does this mean I could go to prison? Why don't they teach us these things properly in school?'
Anna (15)

'I don't like my doctor. He is old-fashioned and is always telling me that nice girls don't have sex. My mum says it's just his way but it makes me uncomfortable. Where else can I go?'
Tina (16)

'I sometimes wonder if it's more bother to seek help than not. I went to my doctor about a discharge and he started asking me all these questions about my sex life. I was so embarrassed I just left.'
Karen (14)

'I have just been told I've got to have an internal examination and I am terrified. I've heard that all the doctors stand round and you have to lie there completely naked. I just don't think I could go through with it.'
Jackie (16)

YOUR LEGAL RIGHTS

Once you are over the age of 16, you are the only one who can say whether or not you want an examination or treatment. This means your parents can't make you do anything you don't want to do. Before this age the law is very ambiguous. It basically states that children under 16 can give or withhold consent as long as they fully understand what the proposed treatment or examination entails. This is at the discretion of the doctor. You cannot be involved in experimental operations and the donation of organs until you are 18 years old.

Teenagers have the same right as adult patients to consult any doctor confidentially. You don't have to go along with your parents and your parents do not have to be present during an examination. However, even though the doctor cannot tell your parents that you have come to the surgery, he or she will undoubtedly try and persuade *you* to tell your parents.

HOW TO GET ON WITH YOUR DOCTOR

Learning how to deal with your doctor can be hard. Lots of people are still rendered silent by the presence of their doctor, whether through fear or awe. The important thing to remember is that doctors are there to help you and not to judge you. You can question anything they say to you. If you don't understand what they are saying or why they have prescribed you something, then you need to speak up. Learn to communicate with your doctor the way you do with your friends and teachers.

The following are all ways of ensuring you keep a healthy relationship with your doctor.

- Be as clear as you can. Your doctor may ask you questions that seem nosy, silly or useless. Don't be vague about your answers: they are important. Otherwise the doctor wouldn't bother to ask you.
- Don't lie. This can be dangerous for your health.

Doctors are there to help you and they can only do this if you tell them all the facts.

- Don't be afraid to ask for help for the problems that aren't physical; for example, depression. If you need to talk to someone like a counsellor, ask your doctor to refer (i.e. send) you to one.
- Ask about anything you don't understand, no matter how stupid you may think your questions are.

Changing your GP/doctor

It can be hard to see your childhood doctor as someone who can help you with your adult problems. Perhaps you feel he or she may 'disapprove' or will tell your parents. Or maybe you want to change to a female doctor because you are too embarrassed to have a male doctor examine your body. If this is the case, don't worry. There is nothing wrong with this; lots of women do it. However, I will just say that the great majority of doctors will not feel any sexual interest while examining you. Doctors are trained professionals who see dozens of bodies a week and won't be shocked, embarrassed or suggestive about anything you've got to show them.

If you are at all worried about what you may have to do during an examination you can always have a chat with your doctor and ask all the questions that worry you before you go any further. If you still don't feel comfortable then you can change GPs, either to a different doctor within that surgery or to another surgery altogether.

You can change your GP for any reason whatsoever,

and you don't have to tell anyone why. All you have to do is find another surgery and ask them to take you on. And how do you choose a doctor? Start by asking your friends, school nurse, parents or an adult you trust for a recommendation. As long as you live in the same area as the doctor you want to change to and they have some space on their books, there should be no problem. When you find a doctor you like, just go there (take along your medical card if you have one) and ask to be taken on.

For details of how to find a dentist in your area, see page 119.

Where to go if you don't want to see your GP

Brook Advisory Centres

Brook Advisory Centres were founded in London in 1964 in response to the fact that unmarried people who wanted contraceptive advice and information had nowhere to go. In 1967 the NHS (Family Planning) Act permitted local authorities to give contraceptive advice to the unmarried for the first time and Brook pledged to see under 16s. However it wasn't until 1974 that contraception became free to everyone.

Brook now offers young people free, confidential birth control advice and can also help with emotional and sexual problems. No matter what your reason for going to Brook, everything you discuss will be private and confidential. Even if your worries have nothing to do with contraception and you need to talk about a relationship or your sexual feelings this is the place to go. So if you need immediate information about contraception, pregnancy testing, abortion, sexually transmitted diseases or emergency after-sex contraception, this is the place for you. For further information, contact Brook Advisory Centres (see 'Resources').

Family Planning Clinics

Family planning is free to everyone on the National Health Service. When you need contraception or advice there are a number of places you can go:

- Your GP
- A family planning clinic
- A youth clinic

The Family Planning Association provides a national information and advice service on contraception, safer sex and reproductive health care. They also have details of where your local clinics are, though they do not run them. See 'Resources' for how to contact them. If you want to find your nearest family planning doctor or clinic you can also look in your local directory or your local library. Most chemists can also provide this information. Some family planning clinics also run special young people's sessions (youth clinics). Again, everything that goes on at these clinics is completely confidential.

INTERNAL EXAMINATIONS

The possibility of this kind of examination makes most women keep their pains, discharges and worries to themselves. However it is a very important examination. Just like a dentist can't do anything about your teeth if you don't open your mouth, a doctor can't make sure you're healthy inside without checking your genital region. Of course, the thought of having an 'internal' examination makes most people wince. In fact many women would rather run a 200 mile marathon than face an internal examination. Often this is because they don't know what to expect and are put off by horror stories from their friends.

Internals are important for a number of reasons. First, as your reproductive organs are inside your body, a doctor has to check inside your vagina to make sure everything is OK. It is also the only way a doctor can discover if you have any sexual infections. Remember, you can ask for a female doctor to do the examination. And remember to book your appointment at a time when you don't have your period.

Before a doctor examines you, he or she will usually ask you a few questions. The point of these questions is to discover if there are any illnesses that run in the family and whether there are any symptoms you haven't told the doctor about. The questions may seem pointless to you but they are important, so you must answer them honestly. If you are not sure why a particular question is being asked, then ask the doctor why they need to know.

What happens during an examination?

The procedure is simple, private and relatively hassle-free.

- You will be asked to empty your bladder and

remove your pants and the clothes on the lower part of your body. You will then be asked to lie on a couch and raise your knees. This way the doctor can see your vaginal area clearly. It is an embarrassing position to be in but you must remember that your doctor has seen plenty of women in exactly the same position and won't be at all embarrassed.

- The next stage is perhaps the most uncomfortable, especially if you've never used tampons or had sex. This is where the doctor will gently slide two gloved fingers into your vagina. This can feel strange and distressing but it is painless. Just remember to relax as this will make it easier for the doctor to insert his or her fingers. The doctor will usually use his or her other hand to press down on your lower abdomen in order to feel your organs.

- The next thing the doctor may do, especially if you are having a cervical smear, is to use a 'speculum'. This is made of metal or plastic and looks a bit like two long, flat, thin spoons hinged at the handles. The doctor will very gently slide it into your vagina. This may feel uncomfortable but so long as you don't tense your muscles, it will not hurt. With the speculum in place the doctor can see the cervix clearly and can note if there is anything wrong such as cysts or erosion.

- It may seem horrible that two fingers will fit into your vagina (or that a speculum will, for that matter), but remember the vagina is very flexible and its muscles are elastic enough to allow a baby to pass through. The speculum is used to hold the soft walls of the vagina apart, so that the doctor can check that your vagina is healthy.

- While the speculum is in place, the doctor will insert a thin spatula (it resembles an ice-lolly stick) to collect some cells from the surface of your cervix. It's completely painless, as your body sheds cells all the time and your cervix has few nerve endings. This sounds like a long, drawn-out process but it is over pretty quickly.

- Sometimes as part of the examination, the doctor will look at your breasts for signs of any lumps (see also page 49 for breast checks). The majority of these lumps are harmless and nothing needs to be done to them. To check for possible lumps, the doctor will 'palpate' your breasts, by pressing his or her fingers over the whole of your breast area. You may also be asked to raise your arms or put your hands on your waist.

- After an examination you may feel a bit tearful or strange; this is again normal. Internal examinations are very personal and make the majority of women feel vulnerable. This is why it can help to take a friend, who can give you a bit of emotional support. Remember, the first one is always the hardest and after that it really does get easier.

When the examination is over, make sure you ask if anything is wrong, and if you had a cervical smear, ask when and how the results will come. They may be posted to you, or you may have to ring the surgery. Sometimes you will be called in for a re-test either because the first test samples were insufficient or because you may have a minor infection.

SEX EDUCATION AND THE LAW

What sex education are you entitled to?

Amendment 62 on sex education took effect in August 1994. The section has three effects:

- It makes sex education compulsory in all secondary schools, including information about HIV/AIDS and other sexually transmitted diseases.
- It removes from the National Curriculum all reference to HIV/AIDS and sexually transmitted diseases, and to aspects of human sexual behaviour other than the biological ones.
- It gives parents the right to withdraw their children from all or part of sex education lessons where they are not part of the National Curriculum.

What this basically means is that your parents have no say over what you can and can't learn under the National Curriculum, which means they cannot stop you from learning about the scientific aspects of sex, like how babies grow. All schools also now have to be able to teach you about the non-biological aspects of sex, such as how to handle relationships and where to go for help. However, as these topics are not under the National Curriculum, your parents can actually stop you from receiving these lessons. This means you could miss out on vital information on topics such as AIDS/HIV, sexually transmitted diseases, contraception, gay and lesbian issues.

What if your parent withdraws you from sex education?

If your parent withdraws you from sex education, your teachers cannot give you advice on any sexual matter without your parent's consent. However, a teacher can tell you where to seek confidential help (e.g. a local clinic or your GP) as this is not seen as providing sex education but merely giving you information as to where you can legally get advice. These organizations will happily give you any information you need.

Does sex education encourage sex?

According to the World Health Organization, there is no evidence to suggest that sex education leads to increased sexual activity. In fact, sex education can delay or decrease sexual activity and lead to sexually active young people adopting safer practices.

> • In an FPA survey, only 60% of respondents aged 16 and under had been taught about contraception at school.
> • Only 45% of respondents aged 16 and under had been taught about HIV/AIDS.
> • Only 29% of respondents aged 16 and under had been taught about sexually transmitted diseases.
> • 70% of all respondents thought they received too little sex education at school.

• 59% of all respondents thought sex education should start between the ages of 8 and 11.
• 70% of respondents thought their sex education did *not* help them to understand how the opposite sex felt about sex.
• 94% of young people felt their parents should be the main source of sex education, but most got their information from friends and the media.

THE AGE OF CONSENT

Girls cannot legally have sex until they are 16 years old. If a girl under 16 does have sex and is found out, it's the boy and not the girl who can be prosecuted. If couples are the same age or the boy is a year or so older than the girl, it is unlikely a prosecution would take place. But if the man happens to be a lot older than the girl he could receive a prison sentence.

As having sex with a girl under 16 is a criminal offence, a doctor who provides contraception to the couple could be said to be aiding an illegal act, but the British Medical Association says that if a doctor acts in good faith to protect a girl against the potentially harmful effects of intercourse, the doctor would not be acting illegally.

It is important to note here that the age of consent for male homosexuals is 18. Even though homosexuality is not illegal, the law still discriminates against people who are gay.

THE LEGAL POSITION ON CONTRACEPTION

In 1985, the House of Lords established the current legal position in the UK, which states:

'People under 16 who are able to fully understand what is proposed and its implications are competent to consent to medical treatment regardless of age.'

This basically means that doctors have the right to judge whether or not they think you're mature enough to receive contraception before they give it to you. A doctor will judge this on your ability to understand the choices he is offering you and your reasons behind wanting contraception. However, most doctors think that if you're adult enough to ask for contraception, you're adult enough to be given it. Their prime concern is not to give you a lecture on the perils of underage sex but to prevent an unwanted pregnancy or a sexual disease.

Even if your doctor does consider you to be too immature, he or she has to keep your request confidential, and you are still free to go to another doctor or clinic and ask again.

Doctors are also legally obliged to encourage under-16s to inform their parents; however, they cannot force you to tell your parents. If you are at all worried about visiting your family GP, visit a Brook Advisory Centre instead (see 'Resources'). They specialize in counselling and advising young people on contraception and sex.

Confidentiality and contraception

Less than 25% of sexually active girls under 16 seek family planning advice and information. The remaining 75% leave themselves open to pregnancy, AIDS and sexually transmitted diseases because they are afraid that their doctor could not or would not preserve confidentiality regarding their requests for contraception. Remember, all doctors are tied to the confidentiality ruling and this means they *cannot* tell your parents that you've come to see them.

How easy is it to get contraception and advice?

It's easier than you may think. It may be against the law for a boy to have sex with a girl under 16, but it is not illegal for anyone to use or buy contraceptives if they are under 16. Condoms are readily available from chemists, supermarkets and even some record stores. They are distributed free at Family Planning Clinics and Brook Advisory Centres, where you can also get advice on all forms of contraception. In addition, information and advice about contraception forms a part of sex education in schools. It's very important to know your full medical history before you go to a clinic or advisory centre. This way they can give you the best contraceptive advice.

PREGNANCY

Every year 200,000 women in Britain find themselves with an unplanned pregnancy. The most obvious sign of pregnancy is a missed period but the best way to find out for sure is to have a pregnancy test. If you think you may be pregnant the first thing to do is to go along to your GP or your nearest clinic and find out for sure if you are pregnant. Brook Advisory Centres provide completely confidential free pregnancy testing and counselling.

If you are pregnant there are a number of choices available to you. The decision is a hard one to make, but it is your decision and no one can force you to do something you don't want to do. Even if you are under 16 years old, no one can make you either have an abortion or keep the baby if you don't want to. If you do decide to go ahead with the pregnancy, there are many good books available on the subject, as well as counselling and advice from the organizations listed at the end of this chapter.

Keeping the baby

If this what you want to do, go and see your GP as soon as possible. It is very important for you to have proper pre-natal care especially if you are in a difficult situation at home. Your GP can also help and advise you if you need extra support, for example with housing.

Abortion

(See also section on abortion in chapter 2.) Abortions have been legal in this country since the 1967 Abortion Act. But they are not available simply on request. In order to get an abortion, two doctors must agree that you have 'grounds' for an abortion. If you want an abortion on the NHS, one of those doctors would generally be your GP and the other would be the doctor at the local hospital who will be in charge of the actual abortion. If you decide to have an abortion by one of the abortion charities it can cost up to £250.

You can have an abortion if your doctors agree that your mental or physical health would be at risk if you do not have one. If you don't want to see your GP or if he or she is against abortion then you can either go to a Brook Advisory Centre (they will offer you advice on where to go for an abortion) or go straight to a pregnancy advisory service.

If you are under 16 years old it is very unlikely that a doctor will agree to do an abortion without parental consent. It is also important to know that an abortion *cannot* be done against your wishes even if you are under 16. If you want an abortion and your parents don't want you to have one, then you can ask a social worker to help you. If an agreement cannot be reached, a court ruling in your favour will usually be reached.

For further information on abortion, contact BPAS, the British Pregnancy Advisory Service (see 'Resources'), or one of the organizations listed below.

Adoption

Some girls decide that they can't go through with an abortion and opt for adoption instead. If you choose to do this then you need to get in touch with the Adoption and Fostering section of your local Social Services Department (look for the number in the phone book). Couples are selected very carefully to make sure they will make good parents so your child has every chance of going to a good home. For further information contact BAAF, the British Agencies for Adoption and Fostering (see 'Resources').

Fostering

You may find you want to look after your baby but are having problems with housing or money. In this case it may be possible to have your baby fostered for a while. This means placing your child temporarily with a family selected by the Social Services. However, it can sometimes be hard for young single mothers to then get their children back from the Social Services as they have to prove they can be caring and responsible parents and have overcome the problems that first led them to putting their child in foster care. For further information contact NFCA, the National Foster Care Association (see 'Resources').

Further information
For more information and counselling on pregnancy and abortion, contact one of the following: the British Pregnancy Advisory Service, the Pregnancy Advisory Service, Marie Stopes International, or the Family Planning Association (see 'Resources').

• According to a Brook advisory pamphlet, couples are twice as likely to break up if one or both partners is under 20, and a baby was on the way when they got married.

- One in eight teenage mothers surveyed by the FPA and Middlesex University said that they only discussed contraception with their parents after they became pregnant.
- One in five young people have experienced sexual intercourse before the age of 16.
- UK teenage pregnancy rates are the highest in Western Europe and the second-highest in the western world after America, where the rate is 117 per 1,000 girls.
- In the Netherlands, assurance of confidentiality in all contraceptive services has been a key factor in reducing the teenage pregnancy rate to the lowest of all developed countries: only 4 per 1,000 fall pregnant.
- The average age of first sexual experience in the UK is 14 years old; the average age of first intercourse is 17 years old.
- 7,800 girls under 16 became pregnant in 1994.
- A third of the 17,000 people known to have HIV in Britain are under 24 years old. Since the incubation period for the virus is thought to be 8 years most would have become infected as teenagers.
- In Denmark school nurses hand out one million free condoms every year.
- Of the estimated 52,000 sexually active 15-year-old females in England in 1991, only 18,000 visited family planning clinics.
- In England and Wales in 1990, one in every 100 young women aged 13–15 became pregnant.

Chapter Two

SEXUAL HEALTH

Sexual health is a tricky subject for most people, mainly because if there is something wrong 'down below' it automatically becomes too embarrassing to mention to anyone. After all, who wants to hear about your strange itches and rashes? Who wants to know that something odd is happening every time you go to the toilet, or that your periods have stopped. All in all it's a scary business. But sexual health should be dealt with in exactly the same way you deal with your general health. Your doctor's not going to be shocked when you say you've got a sore throat, and in the same way he or she is not going to be shocked when you say you've got a weird discharge or strange lump. And they definitely won't be shocked if you tell them you've been having sex.

Doctors see hundreds of women every month with sexual problems and they are not suddenly going to be disgusted or freaked out by something you have got. Don't be put off by internal examinations either (see page 9). They are very important examinations and a doctor can't make sure you're healthy inside without carrying one out. Contrary to popular belief they don't take hours to perform and they aren't painful, just uncomfortable.

Of course, sexual health is also about sex, and if you're considering sex there are a number of things to consider before you jump into bed with someone. For a start, are you having sex for the right reasons? If you're having sex because . . .

'All my friends are doing it.'

'My boyfriend will leave me if I don't.'

'I'm too old to be a virgin.'

'My best friend says it's brilliant.'

. . . then you're having sex for the wrong reasons. Sex at its best is an expression of love, trust and commitment between two people, and at its worst it's a painful and heartbreaking experience. Sex doesn't always equal love, and vice versa. If you really think you and your boyfriend are ready for sex then do it the right way. This means protecting yourself by using the right contraception, having regular check-ups to make sure you're healthy (this includes cervical smears, and internal examinations), and not being promiscuous. (Sleeping around carries a huge risk: the more lovers you have, the more likely you are to contract a sexual disease – including AIDS.)

Above all, if you think you may be pregnant or have a sexual disease, don't ignore it – because it won't go away. Seek help immediately at your GP, a GUM clinic, Brook Advisory Centre or Family Planning Clinic (see 'Resources').

VAGINAL DISCHARGE

I have this odd discharge in my knickers and I just don't know what to do about it. It's embarrassing and I just can't mention it to my mum. She might think I've been having sex or something.'
Louise (15)

It is quite normal to have a small discharge from the vagina. The secretion has a purpose: to keep the vagina moist and healthy. It is usually clear or slightly milky in texture. When this dries it may turn faintly yellow. At certain times (e.g. during your period or just before it begins, or when you are sexually excited) this discharge may increase.

MASTURBATION

'I feel so guilty when I touch myself. I keep saying I'm not going to do it again but I can't help myself. My friends say it's disgusting so I can't talk to them about it, and my mother says masturbation makes you less sexual.'
Vicky (15)

Contrary to popular belief, masturbation in no way affects your health. It won't make you blind, or cause your hand to fall off, or 'ruin you for proper sex'. If you've never heard the term masturbating it may be because you have heard some of the following instead: wanking, playing with yourself, tossing off, etc. Basically, masturbating means rubbing your sexual organs in order to get yourself sexually excited and/or to give yourself an orgasm.

Women's and men's genitals may look completely different but there are more similarities than you may think. Both men and women masturbate by rubbing (stimulating) a sexual organ that becomes erect during sexual arousal. For women this is the clitoris and for men the penis. As well as exploring these organs, many people find touching other parts of their bodies enjoyable too.

Wanting to explore how your body works and what makes you feel good is a natural part of becoming an adult. Most people discover from a very young age that touching their own sexual organs makes them feel good.

A good thing about masturbating (apart from the obvious) is that it helps you to get to know your own body, how it works and what makes you feel sexually satisfied. This can help you and your partner when you begin a sexual relationship. As for a time limit to masturbation, there is no set pattern for it. For some people it lasts for a few seconds, for others it can last up to an hour. Some people do it once every couple of months, others do it a couple of times a day.

It's also important to remember that although lots of people masturbate, it's perfectly OK not to. Some people never feel the need and this doesn't mean they are frigid or won't ever enjoy sex. Masturbation is just like sex, you should never do it just because everyone else is doing it.

CONTRACEPTION
Contraception and the law

Some people don't use contraception because they can't be bothered. Others because they are afraid they'll 'get caught' and be reported to their parents. The fact is contraception is easier to get than you think. So why risk sex without it?

- It is against the law for a boy to have sex with a

girl who is under 16, but it is not illegal to use or buy contraceptives if you are under 16.

- If you are below the age of consent doctors have the right to judge whether or not they think you're mature enough to receive contraception before they give it to you.
- Even if they refuse to give you contraception, they cannot tell your parents you've asked for it.
- If you are at all worried about visiting your family GP, visit a Brook Advisory Centre instead. They specialize in counselling and advising young people on contraception and sex.

The condom

What is it?

The condom works by stopping sperm getting into the vagina. Condoms resemble long rubber balloons and come rolled up in a packet. They are made from thin latex rubber and are designed to be put over an erect penis before sex. They only come in one size and despite what people say, they will fit any man. In fact, in tests carried out by Durex, condoms have been found to stretch to around a metre long and 50 centimetres wide.

When you open a condom make sure you unroll it the right way. The best way to do it is to squeeze the closed end (the part that looks like a nipple) and roll the condom down over the penis. After sex it's important that the condom is held firmly in place so it doesn't slip off as the penis goes limp.

Advantages

They are very easy to use and to buy. You can buy packs in chemists, supermarkets and other shops. When buying a packet always make sure that it hasn't passed its use-by date and that it carries the British Standards kitemark, as this shows it has been properly tested. You can also obtain condoms free from your nearest Family Planning Clinic or Brook Advisory Centre. Condoms also come in a variety of textures, colours and flavours.

Disadvantages

You have to be careful not to tear or break the condom and you also have to make sure it's put on and taken off properly. Some people think they're not very sexy, but others find that they can be quite fun.

Is it for you?

Yes! It's the easiest form of contraception to use and if used properly will protect you from HIV, pregnancy and sexually transmitted diseases (STDs).

How effective is it?

98% if used properly.

The Pill

What is it?

This is a hormone pill that you swallow. It usually comes in a packet of 21 pills and you take one a day for three weeks, stop for seven days when you usually have a period, and then start a new pack. There are various different types of pill which vary slightly in hormone content and how you take them. For instance, the combined pill contains two hormones, oestrogen and progestogen, while the mini pill contains only progestogen. Both work by either stopping an egg from being released from the ovary or by stopping the fertilized egg from being implanted in the womb. The pill is only available from your GP or a clinic on prescription.

In 1995 news of three (as yet, unpublished) studies caused a scare amongst users of the pill. The studies indicated that certain combined pills containing gestodene and desogestrel were associated with a risk of venous thromboembolism (also known as deep vein thrombosis – blood clots in the leg). However, the risk of this occurring is actually very rare (only 2 in 10,000) and takers of these pills should not panic. (Combined pills containing gestodene or desogestrel include: Mercilon, Marvelon, Femodene, Femodene ED, Minulet, Triadere, Tri-Minulet.)

If you are at all worried see your GP or go to your local Family Planning Clinic, once you have completed your current cycle. **Do not just stop taking the pill. The risk of an unplanned pregnancy is far higher than any risk of thrombosis.**

Advantages
It's simple to use, you take it once a day and it is the most reliable method of contraception. It does not interfere with sex and it often relieves painful periods and PMS.

Disadvantages

The pill offers no protection against AIDS or STDs. If you are on the pill and find yourself getting headaches, or suffering from migraines or any other kind of side effect, you need to go back to your doctor and maybe switch the kind of pill you are on.

Is it for you?

Only if you use it with a condom to make sure you are protected against HIV and STDs.

How effective is it?

99% effective.

The female condom (Femidom)

What is it?

The female condom is just that – a condom for women to wear. It's like a male condom but instead of fitting over *his* penis, it fits into *your* vagina. You put it in just like a tampon by compressing the closed end and inserting it into your vagina. The ring at the open end remains on the outside of your vagina to hold it in place. It is a barrier method of contraception which means it will protect you against pregnancy, HIV and sexually transmitted diseases.

The condom itself looks rather like a long clear plastic bag with a thin ring of plastic at the open end and a thicker one at the closed end. The condom comes in a lubricated package with spermicide and is about seven inches long and three inches wide. It sounds huge but in fact, it's not much bigger than a male condom.

Advantages

With male condoms there's no choice when it goes on and comes off, i.e. it has to go on when he's erect and come off immediately after sex. The female condom, however, can be put in at any time before sex (though it's not recommended that you go out for the evening in one) and taken off any time after sex. It also scores high in the safe sex stakes, and gives the woman more control of contraception than the male condom does. It is also good for people who are allergic to the latex in male condoms because it is made from a different substance called polyurethane.

Disadvantages

As it hangs out of your body, it can look a little unsightly to your boyfriend!

Is it for you?

Well, some women swear by it while others compare it to having sex inside a plastic bag! Apart from that it's easy to use and available from your local chemist.

How effective is it?

98% with careful use.

Morning-after pill (Emergency contraception)

What is it?

This is not a normal method of contraception – it is for emergency use only. Doctors and clinics that supply normal forms of contraception will also supply the morning-after pill. It is a very high dose contraceptive pill (an ordinary pill won't work) that has to be taken within 72 hours of unprotected sex. It is taken in two doses twelve hours apart and works by altering the hormone balance in your body to prevent pregnancy.

Advantages
It is 96% effective in stopping you from becoming pregnant.

Disadvantages
As it contains a high level of hormones it can make you feel very sick. If you're sick you have to go back to your doctor and get another dose and take it all over again.

Is it for you?
Only if you've had unprotected sex or if a condom has split. It is very important to remember that this is not a regular method of contraception – it is an emergency last resort measure.

Other Forms of Contraception

IUD
(Also known as the coil.) This is a small device, usually plastic with copper, that is put into the woman's womb by a doctor. It stops fertilized eggs from settling in the womb. It is no protection against HIV and STDs and can sometimes cause cramps and bleeding. It is usually only given to older women.

Injections

With this method, a hormone is slowly released into the body to stop eggs from being released. It is only offered to women who can't use any other method of contraception.

Safe period (Rhythm method)

This works on the principle that there are certain 'safe' times of the month within your cycle. It is not at all suitable for young women because you have to have extremely regular periods in order to work out your fertile and infertile days.

Diaphragm

Also known as the cap, this is a thin rubber dome that is placed inside the vagina before sex and has to be kept in for up to six hours after. It must be used with a spermicide in order to be effective. Usually only given to older women who can be bothered with the hassle.

Definitely not contraception

Withdrawal

This has been proven time and time again *not* to be reliable and still people think it works. This is the method by which a boy removes his penis from a girl's vagina before he ejaculates. It doesn't work because sperm can and does leak out before ejaculation. This is the method that accounts for the high number of unwanted teenage pregnancies each year.

Douching

Douching is washing out the vagina after sex. It is *not* reliable and possibly even increases the chances of pregnancy. Also causes vaginal infections.

Further information

For confidential information, help and advice, contact Brook Advisory Centres or the Family Planning Association (see 'Resources'). You don't have to be having sex in order to call them. They are there to advise anyone who wants more information regarding sex and contraception, regardless of age or experience.

• Condoms, or sheaths as they were once called, have been used for centuries, as far back as 3,000 BC.

• The average condom stretches to about five feet long and can hold two litres of water.

• A man ejaculates millions of sperms when he orgasms, and they can live for up to eight hours once ejaculated.

• Using a condom with hand cream like Nivea or Vaseline or any sort of oil will make the rubber dissolve in as little as 90 seconds. (If you need some extra wetness, use one of the special creams such as KY jelly or Durex lubricating jelly, or a spermicide.)

• One condom in three is now bought by women.

• Three million people in the UK use condoms as their main method of birth control.

• 140 million condoms are used in the UK each year.

• For every one person making Durex condoms, there are two testing them for quality.

ABORTION AND THE LAW

Abortion (also known as termination) has always been a controversial subject. You may have read about the anti-abortion fanatics in the USA who have murdered eight people (mostly doctors) in their battle to ban abortion. These people, like many people in the UK, believe that abortion is the same as murder and argue against abortion on religious and humane grounds. They claim that an unborn child has as much right to live as a child who has been born.

Others, including the Pro-Choice Movement, believe that abortion is not murder, because a foetus is not a child until it is born. They believe that the foetus is simply a mass of cells and not a fully formed baby when the abortion is carried out, and that it is every woman's right to control her own body and decide whether or not to go through with a pregnancy.

Contrary to popular belief, women who have abortions don't do so easily. Abortion is a difficult and painful decision for every woman who goes through with it, and women can feel guilt about it for many years. It's far better to avoid unwanted pregnancy by careful use of condoms.

Abortion was made legal in the UK in 1967. (Abortion is still illegal in Northern Ireland, except when the woman has a serious medical or psychological problem, or if abnormality of the foetus is detected.) According to the law you can get an abortion if two doctors sign a form agreeing that one or both of the following is true.

- There is a risk of injury to your physical or mental health should the pregnancy continue.

- There is a risk that your baby may be born physically or mentally handicapped.

Whether you go to your GP, a doctor or a clinic, the same thing will happen. You will be asked to explain why you want to terminate your pregnancy. The first doctor will also give you a medical examination to see how many weeks pregnant you are. If the doctor agrees to an abortion, an appointment will be made with a second doctor at a hospital or a clinic. The second doctor will do the same as the first. If this doctor agrees, you will be given a date and time for the operation.

If you are pregnant and want an abortion, seek professional help – don't attempt anything yourself. Hot baths, taking pills, drinking loads of alcohol, jumping down the stairs or pretending it isn't happening doesn't help or solve anything.

Under-16s and abortion

If you are under 16 years of age it is extremely unlikely that a doctor will allow you to have an abortion without your parents' consent. An abortion, like any other operation, comes with risks and this is why your parents' consent is needed. Even if you decide to have a private abortion, you will also need your parents' permission. If a doctor says no to an abortion for his or her own reasons, you are still entitled to go to another doctor. If your doctor won't let you have an abortion on the NHS then go and see a doctor at an abortion charity such as Marie Stopes Clinics, PAS (Pregnancy Advisory Service) or BPAS (British Pregnancy Advisory Service). Some people prefer these places, as an abortion is less hassle here, though they have to charge at least £200 for an abortion to cover their costs.

What happens during an abortion

The most common method used in an abortion is Vacuum Aspiration. This is where the contents of your womb are gently sucked out. It's relatively painless and is carried out under local or general anaesthetic. You may suffer from cramps and bleeding when you get home. Most places now work on an out-patient basis which means you'll be able to go home after a couple of hours.

If you have an abortion after 12 weeks it will always be done under general anaesthetic and you usually have to stay overnight. This method is called a D&C (dilation and curettage) – and involves the contents of your womb being scraped out.

Later abortions after 16 weeks are very unpleasant because they are induced by drugs, meaning you go into a mini-labour so that the womb contracts and its contents are pushed out. After reading all this you should be more convinced than ever to avoid unwanted pregnancy by careful use of contraception.

The abortion pill (RU486)

This is now available in the UK to women who are less than nine weeks pregnant. It is actually a course of treatment using two drugs to induce a miscarriage in early pregnancy. It is an alternative to surgical abortion and is sometimes known as medical abortion. This basically means you don't have to go into hospital.

The pill works in two stages. First you have to go along to a clinic and take three RU486 pills. These pills work by blocking the effects of progesterone, the hormone responsible for sustaining a pregnancy in your womb. When this hormone is blocked by RU486, the pregnancy will detach from your womb.

Two days after taking this pill you have to go back to the clinic and this time insert a pessary into your vagina (a simple process rather like inserting a tampon). This pessary contains a drug called prostaglandin which will cause your womb to contract and expel the pregnancy. You then have to go back to the clinic 10 days later to make sure the pill has worked.

What happens first?

Before anything happens a trained counsellor at the clinic will talk with you, give you information and answer any questions, queries or worries you may have regarding your pregnancy options. If you then decide to have a medical abortion (RU486) you will see two doctors, as required by the Abortion Act, who will decide if this method is suitable for you.

How long does this treatment take?

The first visit will take two hours, and the next visit six to seven hours. At the first treatment the doctor will counsel you and give you a medical examination before giving you the pills to take. If you are sick the pills won't be effective and you may be asked to have a traditional surgical treatment instead.

At the second visit a pessary will be inserted (you can do it or a nurse will do it for you). Most women find that they will then develop severe cramps and pains very similar to period pains. This happens over the next four to six hours and a miscarriage will usually occur at this time while you are at the clinic.

Does it hurt?

Unfortunately, yes! It is like having very bad period pains; but you will be given painkillers to help you cope with the pain. You may also find that you feel quite sick and nauseous. You also need to be prepared for a certain amount of bleeding and discomfort at the second visit. It is strongly suggested that you visit the clinic with a friend or relative, especially for the second visit.

Post-abortion feelings

Any decision to have an abortion is unlikely to be an easy one. In fact, no matter how sure you are that you want an abortion and no matter how relieved you are that your pregnancy has been terminated, you are bound to have confused feelings later. Research has also shown that girls experience different levels of distress for varying lengths of time after an abortion.

'Even though I'm sure I've done the right thing I still feel that I have lost something – a part of me that I can't get back.'
Sue (16)

'I don't feel anything, just numbness and emptiness.'
Karen (15)

'Sometimes I just burst into tears for no reason. I keep thinking I've done something wrong, even though I know I haven't.'
Keighley (15)

'Whenever something bad happens to me I think it's God punishing me for the abortion. I feel terrible all the time.'
Lucy (15)

These are just some of the normal feelings girls go through after an abortion. The large majority of women deal with this by talking to a counsellor. There are now a number of post-abortion counselling places where you can go and talk to a counsellor one-to-one. Any woman can go along and get counselling no matter how long ago she had her abortion.

Post-abortion counselling is now available through Brook Advisory Centres and Marie Stopes Health Clinics (see 'Resources' for how to contact your nearest clinic).

Further information
For more information on RU486 and abortion, contact Marie Stopes International (see 'Resources' again).

• Every year about 160,000 abortions are carried out in Britain – nearly a fifth of them on girls in their teens.
• About one in five pregnancies end in abortion.

VAGINAL INFECTIONS AND SEXUALLY TRANSMITTED DISEASES

A certain amount of vaginal discharge is normal. However, if you have a thick discharge that itches and/ or smells, or if you feel uncomfortable when going to the toilet, you must see your doctor. It's very easy to get an infection because the vaginal, anal and urinary openings are all very close together. Germs that are harmless in one opening can spread to another and become harmful. Also because the external genital organs have warm, moist parts, germs can breed there if you don't wash regularly.

Always wash daily, and try not to use perfumed soap. Vaginal deodorants are also a no-no: they are unnecessary and can lead to infections. Pants with a cotton gusset are best as they will absorb perspiration and secretions.

Sexual infections are usually known as STDs and anyone can get them. If you're going to have sex then make sure you have safe sex: always use a condom as it will protect you from AIDS, STDs and unwanted pregnancy. If you notice any of the following, seek help from a genito-urinary medicine clinic.

- Strange discharge.
- Pain when you go to the toilet.
- Blood when you go to the toilet.
- Bumps or pinkish, cauliflower-like lumps on your genital area.
- Any odd or sore rashes in your genital area.

If you think you may have a sexually transmitted disease you must go to a special clinic that deals with vaginal infections. These clinics are known as Genito-urinary medicine clinics (GUM clinics) or Special clinics, or VD (venereal disease) clinics. Your GP or local hospital can give you details of your nearest clinic or you can check your local directory.

Everything that happens there is completely confidential and free. Remember, STDs can be treated and cleared up quickly.

Pubic lice

'I know I've caught something because I can see things on my pubic hair and they makes me feel sick. But I can't tell my mum about it. She'll think I've had sex and caught a disease – but I'm still a virgin. What's happening to me?'
Lucy (16)

Pubic lice, also known as crabs, are in fact tiny parasites that live and lay eggs in the pubic area. They are known as an STD but they can also be transmitted through bedding, clothing, towels and toilet seats. If you have severe itching and/or visible eggs on your pubic hair, you may well have caught them. If you think you have, visit your doctor or see your pharmacist for an over-the-counter lotion. Follow the instructions very carefully and also make sure you wash all bedding, towels and clothing in boiling water to destroy all eggs and to ensure you don't infect yourself again.

Cystitis

'I have this awful pain and I have to rush to the toilet, but when I get there nothing much happens but it hurts so much. My doctor says it's cystitis but I have no idea what he means.'
Allie (16)

Cystitis is an infection and/or inflammation of the bladder. It is one of the most common female medical conditions around and affects around 50% of all women at some time in their life. Although not specifically an STD, it can be contracted through sex.

Basically the word cystitis describes a set of symptoms which include:

- A burning, stinging pain when you go to the toilet.
- A constant urge to go to the toilet, which may be so strong that you feel you are going to lose control and wet yourself. In fact, all that passes out are a few drops.
- A dull ache in your abdomen, and backache.
- Darker urine, sometimes with traces of blood.
- Feeling unwell; nauseous, weak and feverish.

What causes cystitis?

Reasons for cystitis attacks vary enormously from woman to woman, but here are some of the main reasons.

- **Infection**. 50% of all cases are caused by germs reaching the urethra (which is usually germ-free) and travelling up to the bladder, where they multiply and irritate the bladder lining. This occurs because a woman's vagina, urethra and anus are so close together and it's very easy for germs to spread.

- **Sex.** Lots of women find that they suffer attacks after having sex. The warm secretions and the swelling tissues caused by sexual arousal encourage the growth of bacterial germs, which can be pushed into the urethra during sex. For many women first-time sex or vigorous sex can cause cystitis.

- **Soaps and bath foams.** Perfumed soaps, bath foams or oils, talc and vaginal deodorants can irritate the sensitive skin around the vagina, acting as triggers for cystitis.

- **Not drinking enough liquid.** Another cause of cystitis is not drinking enough. If you drink frequently you will need to go to the toilet frequently as your urine will be more diluted. This means that harmful germs will be flushed out of your bladder and that there will be less chance of bacteria breeding there. Tea, coffee, fizzy drinks and alcohol all irritate the bladder, so stick to fruit juices and water.

- **Not going to the toilet.** Too many people hang on till the very last minute before going to the toilet, but not urinating regularly can cause problems. Stale urine left in the bladder for too long can make germs multiply.

- **Tight clothes.** Tight jeans, tights, nylon knickers and close-fitting underwear keep the whole genital area damp and stop air from circulating. Again this provides a breeding ground for germs.

How to relieve an attack

It's important to see your doctor when you get cystitis, especially if it's the first time you have had it, if your urine is bloody, if you have a heavy discharge, or if you're not sure what you are suffering from. You can also help relieve an attack by doing the following:

- Drink half a pint of water straight away and every twenty minutes for three hours, as this will help to flush out the germs.
- Avoid alcohol, fizzy drinks and coffee.
- Go to the toilet as much as you need to – don't hold on.
- A hot-water bottle on your tummy and lower back can help relieve the pain.

How to prevent an attack

Prevention is the best cure for cystitis. The following are all things you can include in your daily life to prevent an attack.

- It has been suggested that drinking four pints or more of plain water every day will keep your bladder flushed free of germs. However, if this seems excessive you can help yourself by making sure you drink weak tea. Drink coffee only in the morning and make sure you drink a glass of water at the same time. Dilute your alcoholic drinks, and don't wait until you're thirsty before you drink. Get into the routine of drinking liquid regularly.
- Go to the toilet when you need to go – don't hold it in. Sometimes having a busy life means you

can't be bothered to go through the hassle of going to the toilet. Hanging on to urine causes stress to the bladder and can encourage a cystitis attack.

- Always wipe your bottom front to back to stop the spread of germs from the anus to the urethra.
- Keep the vaginal area clean and make sure you wash it at least once a day.

Thrush

'I have this awful thick discharge and I don't know what it is. It's whitish and very heavy.'
Anona (14)

Like cystitis, thrush is not specifically an STD, though it can be contracted through sex. It is caused by a yeast-like fungus (Candida albicans) that normally lives quite harmlessly on your skin, mouth and in your vagina. If your body is healthy it is kept under control by the presence of certain bacteria. Only when this delicate balance is upset does this fungus grow and multiply and cause discomfort.

This can happen:

- When you take antibiotics. They don't affect yeast directly but they kill other organisms in the body leaving the yeast more room to multiply and cause an infection.
- When you wear tight-fitting clothes. Yeasts flourish in a warm moist environment.
- When you have sex with someone who has it. Although thrush is often caused by the multipli-

cation of yeasts, it is also possible to catch thrush from someone else. It can be carried by men without their having any symptoms.

- When you are unwell, stressed and run down.

The symptoms are:

- Itching, soreness around your vagina and/or anus.
- A thick white discharge that looks like cottage cheese and smells.
- Pain when you go to the toilet.
- Swelling of the vulva.

If you think you have got it then see a doctor. Often he or she can tell straight away by just looking whether or not it is thrush. It can be treated easily by cream and pessaries. A pessary is an almond-shaped tablet which is inserted into the vagina with an applicator (rather like a tampon applicator).

Repeat attacks
Once you have had thrush you will probably recognize it if you get it again. If you do, there is a lot you can do to help yourself:

- Don't have more baths or showers. This can be soothing temporarily but will make the irritation worse.
- Only use water, as soap can irritate thrush.
- You can try using live yoghurt on your vagina. Dip a tampon into the yoghurt and then insert it; this can soothe the irritation.

Cervical cancer and cervical smears

'My mum says when I start having sex I have to have regular cervical smears. Does this mean that sex equals cervical cancer?'
Julie (17)

A cervical smear is a simple and easy test that is performed by your GP or at a family planning clinic in order to detect abnormalities in the cells of the cervix. These abnormal cells are the first warning signs of cervical cancer which, if left untreated, can be fatal. But if detected early, pre-cancerous cells can be treated with complete success. Long before cervical cancer is established there are detectable changes in the cells around the neck of the womb (cervix). Any woman who has had sex could develop cervical cancer but research indicates that your risk is increased if:

- You are over 35.
- You smoke.
- You started having sex at a very early age.
- You've had a lot of partners.
- You have had a sexually transmitted disease.

What does the test involve?

The cervical smear is simple. The doctor will use a 'speculum'. This is made of metal or plastic and looks a bit like two long, flat, thin spoons hinged at the handles. The doctor will very gently slide it into your vagina. Then while the speculum is in place, the doctor will insert a thin spatula (it resembles an ice-lolly stick) to collect some cells from the surface of your cervix.

It's completely painless, as your body sheds cells all the time and your cervix has few nerve endings. It will be over pretty quickly. The scraped cells are smeared at once on to a microscopic slide and sent to a laboratory to be examined under a microscope. If the test is positive you will be sent for further tests in order to detect what's happening to your cervix.

Regular smears

The official recommended interval between tests is five years. However, most experts agree that women should be tested at least once every three years. You should have a test once a year if you are in a high-risk category:

- If you have been infected in the past with genital warts. (It has been found that women who have had the genital wart virus may be more likely to have changes in the cervix which might turn into cancer in later life.)
- If you have had a previous abnormal smear.
- If there is a history of cancer in your family.

Breast cancer and breast checks

'I have this really strange lump in my breast. It's quite fleshy and round and I just can't say anything to anyone about it. I cry every night because I'm convinced it's cancer. What can I do?'
Rebecca (16)

It's a myth that lumps automatically mean cancer. Lumpy breasts are very normal during puberty when your body is growing, and the important thing to realize is that some breasts are naturally more lumpy than others. However, even though breast cancer is very rare below the age of 30, you should learn to be aware of your breasts and examine them regularly. This means checking your breasts every month. Doctors suggest that a good time is just after your period has ended, or at the same time every month.

When you check them, remember you are looking for something unusual for you. So the first time, note the size and shape of your breasts, the look of your nipples and the feel of your breasts. Each time you check them see if they differ at all from the first time. If you notice anything that hurts and/or worries you, get it checked out by your GP. They won't think you're silly or wasting their time, and what's more they can also show you how to check your breasts properly.

The Women's Nationwide Cancer Control Campaign (WNCCC) produces a free leaflet on how to check out your breasts. Send an s.a.e. to the address in 'Resources'.

AIDS

'The whole issue about AIDS is so complicated and confusing. For instance, we're told about AIDS and how not to get it, but what has HIV got to do with it?' *Laura (14)*

AIDS stands for Acquired Immune Deficiency Syndrome:

- **Acquired.** This means it is not in the body to start with.
- **Immune.** Your body's defence system against infection and illness.
- **Deficiency.** This means a lack of something, i.e. in this case the immune system has been weakened.
- **Syndrome.** This means a collection of illnesses originating from one cause, in this case HIV.

Basically this means AIDS is a condition whereby your body's immune system can no longer function properly and fight off illnesses. What this actually means is that people who have AIDS end up dying from illnesses and infections which would not be fatal to a healthy person.

There is no cure for AIDS and until one is found the only way of safeguarding yourself is changing your sexual behaviour. This means limiting your partners and practising safer sex – sex with a condom. Always check the use-by date and make sure it carries the British kitemark triangle (which means it has been tested to UK standards).

HIV

AIDS is caused by a virus called HIV (Human Immuno-deficiency Virus). Just because someone has HIV doesn't automatically mean he or she will develop AIDS, but each person with HIV is capable of transmitting the virus on to other people. Despite the huge amount of research going on, nobody yet knows why HIV makes some people ill while others remain healthy.

How can you catch HIV?

HIV can be caught by having vaginal or anal sex with an infected person. (Note that a person may not know they are carrying HIV and that you can't tell if someone is infected by looking at them.) This is because HIV only survives and is transmitted in body fluids such as blood, vaginal fluids, semen and breast milk.

HIV can be caught by sharing needles and syringes (for injecting drugs or anything else) with an infected person. This is because when anything is injected into the body, a small amount of blood is drawn into the syringe. Therefore, when you use someone else's syringe or needle you are injecting their blood into your body. If they are infected, the virus will go straight into your blood stream.

There have, as yet, been no reported cases of AIDS being contracted through ear piercing or tattooing in the UK. However, you could be at risk if you let someone pierce your ears or tattoo you with an unsterilized needle or a needle that has been shared. In order to be safe make sure you always go to a reputable salon. Most ear-piercing salons now use spring-loaded guns, with the ear being pierced by the sterilized ends of the earring itself. As for tattooing, if you are absolutely convinced this is for you and won't let yourself be persuaded otherwise, then at least make sure you go to a professional tattooist, where all needles are sterilized.

Never let a friend give you a tattoo or pierce your ears – this is a guaranteed way to get an infection.

You cannot catch HIV from:

- Sharing cups or glasses.
- Touching.
- Toilet seats.
- Swimming pools.
- Being coughed or sneezed on.
- Donating blood to the National Blood Transfusion Service (as new sterile needles are always used).
- Receiving a blood transfusion in the UK. The blood is first tested for HIV.
- Kissing. There are traces of HIV found in saliva but you would need to swallow at least a pint of saliva in order to contract it!
- Insect bites.

How to protect yourself

Don't fool yourself into thinking only gay people or people abroad get AIDS. AIDS affects everyone and therefore if you have unprotected sex you are putting yourself at risk. Limiting your number of sexual partners and not injecting drugs will help to save your life. Remember, the more people you have sex with, the more likely you are to have sex with someone who has AIDS. And most importantly – always practise safer sex by using a condom. A condom is the best known protection against AIDS.

HIV tests

This is a free blood test which looks for the presence of antibodies in the blood stream, showing whether the body has been infected with the virus. It takes a while for these antibodies to develop, so if you think you may have been exposed to the disease, it is suggested that you wait three months before having the test, or that you have two tests three months apart. If you want the test, go along to your local STD clinic where testing is done in strictest confidence and will not show on your medical records. The test can even be done under a false name. Note that no one can test you for HIV without your consent.

Further information
For more information contact the National AIDS Helpline or the Terrence Higgins Trust (see 'Resources').

Chapter Three

HEALTHY PERIODS

Common terms

- Periods
- Menstruation
- Time of the month
- On the rag
- Bleeding
- Being on
- The curse

Hearing how some people refer to periods can be off-putting, yet what most people seem to forget is that periods are as natural as breathing. You may be wishing for them to start right now or you may be wishing you hadn't wished quite so hard, but like it or lump it, if you're female it's something you can't avoid for 35 to 40 years of your life.

The whole subject of periods is a complicated and confusing one purely because everyone has a different view about what happens, how it happens and what to do when it does happen. Perhaps you've heard the common myths, like 'boys can tell when you're having one', or 'you can't use tampons if you're a virgin'. Maybe you've heard the ones about the girl who died from bleeding too much, or about blood suddenly gushing out. If you have then you're not alone.

Before I started my periods I was told by a well-meaning friend that when you had your period you had to lie in bed all day. According to her that was the only way to make sure you didn't lose too much blood. A friend's mother also told my friend and me that we could still go swimming when we had our periods because it would stop when we got into water. Unfortunately for my friend, her mother forgot to mention we also had to wear a tampon! Another friend didn't know anything about periods, so when she suddenly started she became hysterical because she thought she was dying. It sounds ridiculous but it's true. Thankfully my mother put me straight on all of these things, so when my periods did start it wasn't a terrifying or scary event.

Periods shouldn't be treated as a 'curse' or a taboo subject – they are the most natural thing in the world. They are a sign that your body is healthy and working properly and a sign that your body is maturing.

Of course periods come with both exciting and unsettling moments. Firstly there's the paraphernalia that comes with it – sanitary towels, tampons, panty pads. Then the sizing of these products – normal, super, super plus, slender, mini, etc. Once you've waded through that, there's pre-menstrual tension, period pain, and the general discomfort to get through. With all this to deal with it's hard to imagine that there will ever be a time that you will treat them as a normal part of your life and not dread them every month. Part of learning how to do this is knowing how to deal with your body as it goes through its changes and what to do when your periods do arrive. If you are prepared for these changes and know what to expect you will also feel more comfortable as each stage happens.

Remember, too, that our bodies sometimes mature faster than our emotions and you may feel like your body is racing ahead of you towards womanhood while you still feel like a child inside. This is normal, natural and perfectly acceptable. You don't need to rush ahead and pretend to be something you're not. The key to growing up happy is to do it at your own pace and in your own way.

YOUR GROWING BODY

'For ages now my body has been changing. My breasts have grown, my pubic hair has grown and I even get a small discharge every month, but still my period hasn't arrived.'
Claire (13)

'All my friends have started and I am now the only one in my class with no periods. I feel like a freak. I am 16 years old and everyone calls me the baby.'
Sue (16)

Despite what other girls may say and do, periods are a personal thing and not something to compete over. The fact is you can't make your periods start any more than you can make them stop. There is no set age to start your periods by; some girls start as young as ten years old and others as late as seventeen years old. The important point is that, whatever age and stage you are at, you are normal. However, there are signs to watch out for, signs that will let you know that your body is gearing up for your periods to begin.

Your breasts will begin to grow – they may even feel itchy or painful at first. Then your body hair will start growing. Don't worry, this doesn't mean you are going to turn into a hairy beast overnight, the hair will mostly grow under your arms and in your pubic region (the area between your legs, at the top). Don't be surprised, but your pubic hair will be different from your normal hair: it is usually thicker and darker and slightly wiry in texture.

You may feel strange twinges in your abdomen and/ or a clear whitish discharge in your knickers. This discharge is normal and shows the lining of your vagina is developing and preparing for the start of your periods. You only need to go and see your doctor if the discharge has a strong smell, or is painful or makes you itch.

As for the rest of your body, you may find yourself getting taller or putting on weight. This is when your body shape will change, you may become curvier and more rounded or longer and leaner. This can be awkward at first and embarrassing, especially if you have relatives who insist on saying things like, 'My, haven't you grown into a big girl?' On the whole most adults can be pretty insensitive when your body is growing and changing – they don't seem to realize you don't want anyone to notice, least of all comment on your strange new shape. If you have to cope with someone who keeps commenting in this way, have a word with your mum or ask them straight out not to embarrass you. The chances are they haven't even realized they are upsetting you.

'What's happening to my body? My skin is spotty, I sweat all the time and I can't seem to control my moods.'
Anne (15)

You may also find you are sweating more than usual; this is because your glands and hormones have become active. As long as you make sure you wear clean clothes and use a good underarm deodorant you'll stay fresh. As for spotty skin, again this is related to all the hormone activity inside your body. Forget those miracle cures that promise to rid you of your spots – they don't work. Just make sure you keep your skin washed and clean and whatever you do, don't pick your spots.

It's important at this stage to try not to panic about your new shape. When our bodies are growing they go through funny stages, and what you see now isn't necessarily what you'll end up with. Puppy fat disappears, lanky limbs become elegant legs and arms, spotty skin clears up and breasts become of relatively equal size. Think of your body as a balloon being slowly inflated. It has to go through various strange stages before it can achieve its perfect shape.

Big breasts, small breasts, lopsided breasts

About a year before your periods begin (sometimes earlier and sometimes later) your breasts will begin to grow. You may not notice it at first because it doesn't just happen overnight. Perhaps you'll notice small bumps growing or some insensitive person will point them out to you. Your nipples will also change shape and colour, often becoming darker and/or pinker. Gradually your breasts will become fuller and rounder. Sometimes, one breast will grow larger than the other or they won't grow very much at all. Again this is natural and normal. A woman's breasts are never identical in size and shape, and if yours look different then that's OK. Often during puberty one will develop faster than the other but the slower one will eventually catch up.

As for breast size, that's usually determined by heredity. If most of the women in your family have small breasts then the chances are high that you will as well. Despite what some miracle adverts may claim, no special creams can enlarge your breast size. But there are exercises that you can do that will affect the pectoral muscles beneath the breasts. These will help to lift your breasts making them seem slightly bigger, but that's all they can do. Breasts are made up of fat and tissue, not muscle, and that's why exercise cannot change their shape.

If you think your breasts are too large and they cause you discomfort, then please see your GP for more advice. Breast reductions can be performed on the NHS for health reasons like back strain.

Bras – where to get measured

It's very important when your breasts are growing to make sure they have the right kind of support. This means getting fitted for a proper bra. Breasts need support so they don't sag and become uncomfortable when you're playing sport, walking or even running for the bus. Getting a high quality, well-fitted bra is important. It is estimated that 90% of women in the UK wear the wrong bra size. If you have a bra that does one of the following then the chances are you're wearing the wrong bra size.

- Does your bra cut into your shoulders?
- Is it uncomfortable round your back?
- Do the straps keep falling down?
- Is there too much or too little space in the cups?

In order to be fitted properly go along to the lingerie section in any department store; most large stores will now fit women for bras. The assistants will measure you correctly and give you a variety of bras to try on, in order to find a type that is right for you. The cup size (AA-FF) is determined by the size of your breasts and the 32/34/36 etc. measurement is determined by measuring under your breasts and around your back.

Some girls swear by sports bras, others by under-wired bras, some by padded bras – try to ignore what your friends say and find one that is right for you. After all you're the one who has to wear it. Above all, don't be embarrassed; and don't worry, no matter what your breast size is there will be a bra that fits you – sizes now cross a huge range from double A cups to double F cups. Remember too that you may need to be measured and re-fitted every six months when your breasts are growing and you are changing shape.

PERIODS, PAIN AND BLEEDING
What happens during a period?

Now your body has got into gear and started the whole process of puberty, the next stage to watch out for is the start of your periods. In order to understand how your period works you first have to understand what your reproductive organs are and what happens with them.

- **Womb (or Uterus).** The womb is an upside-down, pear-shaped organ and it is here that a fertilized egg will grow into a baby and here, therefore, that the tissue lining which eventually becomes your period discharge builds up every month.
- **Cervix.** This means 'neck' and it lies between the vagina and the womb. The blood from the womb passes out through here.
- **Vagina.** The passage leading from the lower part of your womb to the outside of your body. It's a strong passageway, which is capable of passing a baby through, so it's more than big enough to accommodate a tampon.
- **Ovaries.** Women are born with thousands of egg cells in their ovaries. It is just one of these egg cells which is released each month when you start your period. The ovaries usually take it in turns to release an egg each month. The other function of the ovaries is to release the hormones which change your body at puberty.
- **Fallopian tubes.** These connect your ovaries to your womb. It is through these tubes that an egg travels on its way to the womb.

Most girls think that menstruation is a once-a-month thing that happens when you lose blood. In fact it's a continuing cycle involving the release of an egg from your ovaries, the build-up of tissue lining in your womb to accommodate this egg (in cast it is fertilized) and finally the loss of this lining (i.e. the bloody discharge of your period) when the egg isn't fertilized. Your cycle refers to the changes that take place in your body every month. Usually this cycle is 28 days and lasts from the first day of your period to the beginning of your next one.

What sanitary protection?

In the UK over 3,000 million disposable sanitary towels and tampons are used every year. As you can see, it's big business and some unscrupulous people will try to make even more money out of you by persuading you that you need things you don't, such as vaginal deodorants and douches. The fact is no one will be able to tell if you have your period by smell. Menstrual blood does not smell until it comes into contact with the air, and you don't therefore need vaginal deodorants or douches to stay 'fresh'. As long as you wash every day and change your sanitary protection frequently, you will be fine.

However, you do need some form of sanitary protection, and this can be hard to choose. I remember being very confused as I heard stories about not being able to use tampons if you were a virgin and tales of girls who bled through three sanitary towels!

Basically, you can use either sanitary towels or tampons to absorb menstrual blood. Each is as good as the other and what you choose to use depends on you, your lifestyle, and what you're comfortable with.

Sanitary towels

Gone are the days when sanitary towels were so thick you couldn't walk in them. These days towels are so thin no one can even tell you've got one on. You can play sport in them, wear tight-fitting clothes and no one will notice. The one thing you can't do in them is swim.

For those who have never seen a sanitary towel, it is a soft pad with a sticky strip down one side, designed to be worn externally in your pants; the strip sticks to your pants and holds the towel in place. There are many types of towel, in various thicknesses and fibres, e.g. pant liner, regular, super, super plus. You may find you will need to use a thin towel to begin with, and maybe a thicker one as your period gets heavier. If you're not sure which to use check the towel packet and see what it recommends. You may have to experiment with different types of towels before you find one that is completely right for you. It's easy to see when a towel needs to be changed, and used towels can be disposed of either down the toilet (if they are flushable) or in a sanitary bin, or a normal bin if they are well wrapped up. Always check instructions on the packet before you dispose of them.

Tampons

The most important thing to know about tampons is that they have nothing to do with virginity. The myth comes from the idea that the existence of your hymen (a thin layer of skin at the inside entrance to your vagina) was a sign you were still a virgin because the only way it could be broken was by intercourse. The truth is that some girls are born without a hymen, others break theirs without knowing while playing sport or horse-riding – or by inserting a tampon. The only way you can lose your virginity is by having sexual intercourse.

It's also rubbish that a tampon can get lost inside you. The cervix is only as big as a pin head so the tampon has nowhere to go but out the same way it came in once you have inserted it. Also it cannot fall out because once it has been inserted correctly, the walls of the vagina close gently round it and the muscles hold it in place. You do not have to remove it when you go to the toilet because the opening for your bladder (the urethra) is *above* your vagina, not *in* your vagina.

The absolute worst that can happen (and this is rare) is that you cannot remove it. If this happens, don't panic; just go along to your GP, who will remove it for you. Don't be embarrassed; this can happen to anyone at any age and it can be removed literally in seconds.

Tampons come in various sizes and with or without applicators. They are about the size of a small lipstick and made from compressed cotton wool and other natural fibres. Most women use a regular tampon but if you've just started, a mini or slender one will be sufficient. A tampon is placed inside your vagina and absorbs the menstrual blood before it reaches the outside of your body.

Wearing a tampon allows you to do everything you

can do with a towel with the added advantage of being able to go swimming.

Inserting a tampon

The first couple of times you try to insert a tampon (only do this when you have your period) you might fail. This can be due to various things such as tensing up your muscles or being unsure of what you're actually doing. If you have tried and failed, don't give up. Getting the hang of it can be quite hard but you'll get there in the end. Squatting or putting one foot on a chair can help you find the right position. Make sure your hands are washed and then find your vaginal opening. If you insert your finger you'll see that there is plenty of room for a tampon. Then insert the tampon, pushing it gently upwards and backwards as far as it goes. If it is in correctly you shouldn't be able to feel it (though you will feel the string outside the vagina).

It isn't easy to know when a tampon needs changing. Some girls can feel it while others don't. As long as you change it every four hours or sooner you'll be fine. Most tampons are flushable or can be wrapped up and placed in sanitary bins or normal bins.

Toxic Shock Syndrome

TSS or Toxic Shock Syndrome is a very rare but serious illness that has been widely reported in the media after the death of two girls. You may also have noticed warnings about it on the side of your tampon boxes. The fact is, it doesn't just affect women who use tampons but women who don't, men and children too.

Tampons are not the cause of TSS. It is believed to

be caused by toxins produced by a bacteria called Staphylococcus aureus. In certain circumstances, the bacteria can produce a toxin or poison which can cause a sudden fever, vomiting, diarrhoea, a sunburn-type rash, dizziness, or fainting. Between 1985 and 1990 there were 18 identified cases out of a population of 59 million people. Only half of these cases were associated with women using tampons.

Research has suggested that the risk of tampon-related TSS is linked to tampon absorbency. For this reason women are advised to use low absorbency tampons and to change their tampon as often as directed on the pack. Also it is suggested that you consider using pads at night and tampons during the day.

If TSS is suspected you should remove your tampon and go immediately to your doctor.

Working out your cycle

Though the average length of a cycle is 28 days, it varies greatly from person to person. Some girls can have cycles as long as 50 days or as short as 20 days. If you want to work out when your next period is due, count forward 28 days from the first day of your period. (At the beginning you won't know the length of your cycle, so start with the average of 28 days.) Mark down the date, and do the same the next month and the next month. Eventually you'll start to see a pattern between your calculations and when your next period begins. You may be spot on or it may be less or more than 28 days.

Why do I get a discharge before my period?

Discharges before your periods are quite normal. A whitish discharge shows that the lining of your vagina is being kept moist whereas a brown discharge just shows that your period is about to begin. It's important, however, to keep a check on discharges. If your discharge is at all thick, or strange in colour or smell, or if it makes you itch, you must go and see your doctor. You could have an infection or be allergic to something, and only your doctor will be able to tell you and clear it up for you.

PMS (Pre-Menstrual Syndrome)

For years people thought PMS (previously known as PMT – Pre-Menstrual Tension) was some kind of imaginary illness that existed only in women's heads. These days it is recognized that 90% of women have some kind of pre-menstrual symptoms. PMS happens before a period, and can last from three days to two weeks.

Some common symptoms are: tearfulness, bloating, weight gain, spots, mood swings, depression, headaches, sugar cravings, irritation, clumsiness, constipation, and anxiety. No one is quite sure why PMS occurs, but it is agreed that it is due to a hormone imbalance.

What you can do

First you have to check how PMS affects you. This means keeping a note of what happens and when. You can then help yourself by changing what you eat, how much exercise you take and how you relax.

- Caffeine is known to make PMS worse, so don't drink lots of fizzy drinks, tea or coffee.
- Alcohol and smoking also make PMS worse.
- Vitamins such as B6 can help with depression and fluid retention. B6 can be found in meat, fish, whole grains and pulses and bananas.
- Make sure you have a balanced healthy diet that is low in salt and sugar and has lots of fresh fruit and vegetables. This will help to alleviate sugar cravings.
- Experts suggest eating small meals every three hours (during waking hours). The aim is to maintain a steady blood sugar level throughout the day.
- Regular exercise can help alleviate PMS.

Don't expect overnight cures but if your symptoms really don't get better and PMS is making your life hard then see your GP for further help.

Period pain

This is different from PMS because it occurs *during* your period in the form of severe cramps and pains in the abdomen and back. This pain is known as dysmenorrhoea and can sometimes be so bad that you can be sick, vomit or even faint. This sort of pain affects 50% of all women. The pain is caused by muscle spasms in the womb. In young women it is thought to be because the body produces too much of one hormone called prostaglandin which causes contractions in the womb. In some women its effect can be like a mini-labour. Luckily, unlike PMS, period pain does get better as you get older.

What you can do

In mild cases you can take painkillers. See your local pharmacist or chemist to find the best painkiller for you. Some girls find hot baths and a hot-water bottle can alleviate the cramps. As can curling up in bed.

Exercise is really the most helpful thing to do, even though it's the last thing you probably want to attempt. Exercise causes your body to release substances called endorphins which are the body's natural painkiller and which alleviate period cramps.

If your pains are so bad that you can't cope with your daily life, again see your GP, who will be able to help.

Irregular periods

In the early days of your periods you may find that you have a period and then don't get another for a couple of months. This is normal; periods are often irregular in the beginning. It's important to remember that our bodies are delicate and a variety of things can affect their routine. Periods can therefore stop due to stress, illness, worry, exams or excessive weight loss.

Another reason why your period is irregular at first is because it can take up to two years for your body to start ovulating. This may slightly confuse you. After all, we've already said that a period is caused by the discharge of an unfertilized egg and its lining in the womb. The nitty-gritty facts are that the hormone oestrogen is responsible for the shedding of your womb lining, while the hormone progesterone triggers the release of the egg. During puberty there is a slight hormone imbalance whereby there is not enough progesterone to release an egg but there is enough oestrogen to build up a womb lining and shed it. Over time this imbalance corrects itself and your periods regulate.

How much blood will I lose?

The amount of blood lost varies from girl to girl but despite what it may look and feel like, you're not losing pints of it during a period. Some people say you lose two teaspoonfuls, others an eggcupful – and this is about right. It often looks more and feels more than this especially if you are wearing sanitary towels because the blood spreads out over the towel. Another factor to remember is that you are also losing various fluids and tissue that make up the womb lining so altogether the period may seem very heavy.

The way in which different people bleed will also vary. Some women bleed heavily for the first three days then have hardly anything for the last day. Others find it's slow at first and then that it builds up on the last couple of days. The pattern of your period is unique to you, and you should take little notice of what people say should and shouldn't happen. If you are at all worried about the amount you are bleeding, the lack of your periods or the length of your cycle, see your GP, who will be able to put your mind at rest straight away.

Heavy periods

It's hard to say what a heavy flow is if you have just started and your periods haven't regulated yet. The amount of fluid you lose is related to how thickly the lining of your womb grows. If you notice your blood flow suddenly increasing and you are worried, see your GP. Heavy periods can be caused by anything from stress and worry to illnesses such as endometriosis (a condition where tissue is found elsewhere than the lining of the womb) and pelvic inflammatory disease (a pelvic infection). These can affect teenagers but are more common in older women.

Why do I get my period at the same time as my friends and sister?

Women working or living together, and/or who are close friends may find that a strange phenomenon of synchronization occurs. Slowly, over a period of months, you may find that your cycles lengthen or shorten until your periods and those of your friends become synchronized, i.e. they happen at the same time. Scientists believe this change is brought about by pheromones (chemicals we are unaware of but which our brains register). These chemicals alter our hormonal patterns so that our periods synchronize. Though no one is quite sure why this occurs, it could well date from prehistoric times when it was more favourable to have all the females in one group be fertile at the same time.

Further information
For more information on periods, contact PREMSOC (the Pre-Menstrual Society), the Women's Nutritional Advisory Service or the Toxic Shock Syndrome Information Service (see 'Resources').

• There are 14 million menstruating women in the UK.

• Approximately 10 million women (i.e. over 70%) use tampons during their period.

• More than 1.3 billion tampons are used each year in the UK.

• More than 115 billion Tampax tampons have been manufactured and sold worldwide since their introduction in 1936.

• A woman may have over 500 periods in her life. Added together, she could spend six and a half years of her life menstruating.

• During the 1850s the average age for experiencing the first period was 17; today it is 12.5. This is due to better health care and a healthy diet.

• A woman is born with about 250,000 to 400,000 immature eggs (ova) in each ovary which lie dormant until puberty.

• The reason why some may think that using tampons means you're no longer a virgin could be that in 1948 the General Medical Council ordered that every Tampax packet should carry the warning that internal tampons were unsuitable for unmarried women!

Chapter Four

STAYING HEALTHY

What does being healthy mean to you? Does it mean weighing seven stone and looking like a supermodel? Does it mean exercising every day for two hours and feeling guilty when you have a chocolate bar? Does it mean feeling bad every time you think about food? I hope not!

Staying and being healthy is about more than food. It's about having a positive body image and liking yourself. We all have ugly days. Days when our hair won't go right, our stomachs look too big and we think we're the most revolting thing on earth. But then we should also have days when we feel gorgeous and good about ourselves. If the ugly kind of day describes your life all the time then you need to reassess the way you think about yourself. Imagining that your life would be perfect if you were thinner, taller etc. is a myth. I know plenty of girls who put their health at risk by splashing out on expensive plastic surgery techniques to 'improve' their looks or dieting like crazy for that ideal figure, only to find out that despite their new-found looks they still felt the same about themselves. It's hardly surprising; after all, if you think you're worthless on the inside, just improving the outside is like sticking a plaster on a gunshot wound. It doesn't make the slightest bit of difference.

It's hard to believe that being beautiful is an internal not external impression when the media constantly depicts images of what beauty is and isn't. However, if we were to believe all we saw on TV, we'd think that to be an attractive woman we'd have to be thin, tall, preferably blonde and ultimately helpless. But then we'd also have to believe that all men were strong, super-intelligent, rich and sensitive – and of course we don't believe that. Attractiveness is a subjective thing and no matter what you might think, beauty is definitely in the eye of the beholder. Thankfully we all find different things and different people attractive. If we didn't where would the human race be?

If you're still not convinced, ask yourself the following questions. Do you judge people on how much they weigh? Do you pick your friends by how thin and pretty they are? I doubt it. So why judge yourself in such a harsh way? Staying healthy means accepting that you're never going to be a six foot tall super-model-type, but that you can be happy and healthy no matter what you look like.

HEALTHY EATING

'What is cholesterol? I hear about it all the time and how you have to watch it, but I'm not sure what it is.'
Sue (16)

'Why are people always saying fat, sugar and salt are bad for you? How are you meant to cut them all out of your diet? It's so confusing – surely we need them as much as anything else?'
Tracey (15)

Healthy eating is one of the most important ways we

can help ourselves to feel well. It doesn't mean cutting out all your favourite foods or buying more expensive foods. It doesn't even mean worrying about what you eat. Healthy eating means just changing your attitude to food: find healthier ways to cook food, snack on different things, and treat yourself occasionally. To stay healthy we need a good mix of food. Different foods supply different mixtures of minerals, vitamins and nutrients for our body, so no single food can supply all that we need.

Nutritional requirements increase as we reach adolescence due to rapid changes in our height and weight. This is known as the growth spurt and it usually begins when we are about 10 years old. During it, an average of 23 cm is added to our height and 20–26 kg to our weight. Before this time a girl's average body fat is 18%, but during adolescence it increases to 28%. Therefore, the estimated energy requirements per day also go up. For girls aged 11–14 years, at least 2,000 calories a day need to be consumed and for girls aged 14–18 years at least 2,110 calories.

Over 50% of people in the UK are overweight, mainly because they eat the wrong types of food and don't exercise. Body weight is determined by the amount of energy eaten compared to the amount of energy the body uses. This means surplus energy from food and drink is stored in our bodies as fat. Therefore, the only guaranteed way to lose weight is **eat less and exercise more**.

Forget the miracle diets which promise you will lose 5 lbs a week – the sensible amount to lose is 1–2 lbs. Weight loss can be maintained after dieting by exercising, eating a healthy balanced diet, not skipping meals and eating plenty of fresh fruit and vegetables.

So what exactly is healthy eating? Well, healthy eating doesn't mean eating less of everything. It means maintaining a healthy attitude to food and not labelling some foods bad and others as good. Here's what you can do to make sure your diet stays healthy.

Cut down on fat, salt and sugar

Fat

The fat in our food is concentrated energy (measured in calories). We need this energy for growth, to keep our bodies working properly and to enable us to do the things we want to do. Our bodies convert all the food we eat into energy. If too much energy is consumed they convert the excess into excess fat. Ideally one third of calories consumed should be converted into fat.

Fats can be unsaturated or saturated. Saturated fat comes from animal fats and tends to be hard; unsaturated fat is found in vegetables and fish oils and tends to be softer. This fat is also known as polyunsaturates and monounsaturates.

It is recommended that saturates should be replaced with unsaturates; the easiest way to do this is to eat low-fat products. One in four people die from heart disease in the UK and a diet high in saturated fat is one of the main causes of heart disease.

Salt

Salt is something that occurs naturally in our food. It is made up of 40% sodium and 60% chloride and plays an important role in controlling the fluid balance in our bodies. It also works to make sure our muscles and nerves work properly. However, it is thought that too much salt can lead to high blood pressure and may therefore make a person more susceptible to heart attacks. The amount of salt we actually need is about 1–1.2 grams per day (¾ of a teaspoon). This is consumed naturally without adding extra salt to food.

Cutting down on salt in food is easy because all you have to do is stop adding it. It will taste odd at first but your taste buds will quickly adjust and the natural flavour of food will come out instead. Avoid eating too many crisps, salted nuts and other salty snacks.

Sugar

Carbohydrates are divided into two types – sugar and starch. A healthy diet is one that has more starchy carbohydrates (which are very good for you) and less sugars. Starch is found in bread, cereals, pasta, rice and some fruits. Sugars, meanwhile, are found in syrup, jam, treacle, honey, raw cane sugar, glucose, dextrose and fructose (check labels to see) and fizzy drinks. None of these sugars have any nutrients and are not necessary for your body. It is important to cut down on sugar because while it does give you energy, it also causes tooth decay and weight gain, as excess sugar which we do not burn up is converted into fat and stored. Cut down by using low sugar products, or artificial sweeteners.

Reduce cholesterol levels

Cholesterol is a fatty substance that is found naturally in all people. It is essential to a number of body processes such as the formation of hormones and body cells. Cholesterol is also an important ingredient of bile which aids the digestion of fatty foods in our bodies. There is so much talk about cholesterol because even though it is essential to sustain life, too much in the blood can lead to serious health problems.

Very high cholesterol intakes lead to high blood cholesterol levels which in turn lead to a build-up on the walls of your arteries and can lead to heart attacks. Cholesterol is found in saturated fats and fatty products such as dairy food, biscuits, cakes, eggs and sausages, so cutting down on your intake of these things can help.

If you are at all worried then visit your doctor or chemist, who can measure your blood cholesterol and give you advice on how to reduce your cholesterol levels.

How to reduce your blood cholesterol level

- Change to semi-skimmed or skimmed milk rather than full cream milk.
- Exercise at least three times a week.
- Use low-fat spreads rather than butter.
- Eat low-fat cheeses.
- Eat more fish and lean meat.
- Grill foods instead of frying them.
- Avoid junk food.

Eat more fibre-rich food

Fibre is the name for a group of carbohydrates like beans, brown bread, brown rice, wholemeal pasta and vegetables. Many people think rice, pasta and bread are fattening, but it's what you put on top of them that makes them fattening. These foods are rich in fibre and very important for good health. They help prevent constipation, they fill you up and can help protect you against bowel problems including cancer of the bowel – which is one of the most common cancers in Britain. More ways to get more fibre in your diet are to eat more beans (including baked beans), eat more potatoes and try to eat at least one piece of fruit and a bowl of cereal a day.

Eat lots of fruit and vegetables and avoid junk food

Fruit and vegetables have a variety of nutrients, vitamins and minerals stored within them, and are therefore a necessary part of a balanced diet. The fresher and more raw the vegetable or fruit the better it is for you. However, frozen vegetables are good for you too, as are some canned foods such as tinned tomatoes and baked beans.

Further information
For more information on healthy eating contact the British Nutrition Foundation or Foodsense (see 'Resources').

- 85% of women in the US are thought to have some kind of dysfunctional relationship with food.
- 34% of young adults think that healthy foods are 'too boring'.
- On average children get a third of their energy intake from biscuits, sweets, crisps and cakes.
- Children spend more than £220 million a year on sweets and snacks on their way to and from secondary schools.

SELF-IMAGE

How you feel about yourself is more important than how much you weigh. What do you see when you look in the mirror? Do you see a body you love or loathe? The chances are you probably hate bits of it, love a couple of other bits and cope with the rest. However, if you are not doing the things you want because of how you feel about yourself, then you need to consider changing your attitude to yourself and improving your self-esteem.

For some people looking in the mirror can be a nightmare. It can make them feel depressed, miserable, anxious and even suicidal. To check your image ask yourself the following:

- Do you avoid looking at your reflection?
- Do you feel afraid to weigh yourself?
- Do you always ask for reassurance that you look OK?
- Do you stay in because of the way you look?

- Do you feel uncomfortable about letting people see your body?

If you score more than one 'yes', then you have a problem with your body image and you need to do something about it. Changing the way you think about food is a start. It's a well known fact that denying yourself the things you like makes you crave them. A little of what you like is far better for your mental state than you might think. Hard as it is, don't deny yourself life just because you are not at your ideal weight. Don't wait until you are slim to go out and have a good time/ get a boyfriend/ buy new clothes/ be happy. You can have and be all those things right now. Concentrate on being positive about yourself and your self-esteem will improve.

Having a good body image is important because it makes up a vital part of your self-confidence. If you hate the way you look, then you won't project yourself in a positive way to people you meet. If you don't like yourself, you can't expect anyone else to like you back. Learning to respect yourself, warts and all, is a way of saying, 'I'm a great person. I'm worth knowing.' You don't have to make excuses for yourself or what you look like; being happy doesn't mean you have to be a perfect size 10. It means you just have to be yourself and like yourself.

Dieting

'I hear about so many different diets that I'm not sure which one to go on. I don't even know what some of them are. For instance, what's food combining? Or

meal replacements? Are they healthy ways to lose weight?'
Helen (16)

'My friends and I are all calorie-obsessed. I can't eat anything any more without checking the label and making sure it fits into my 1,000-calorie-a-day diet. It's awful – I feel guilty if I eat something bad for me, and yet I crave it if I don't. What's wrong with me?'
Sarah (17)

The slimming industry is worth £1 billion a year – go into any bookshop and you'll see a huge section on dieting. There'll be books that promise you instant weight loss and instant inch loss if only you do x, y and z. Others that will say you can cut out one thing and all your excess weight will miraculously fall off. There's even a book that promises that eating just junk food can help you to lose weight!

Go into any chemist and you'll see shelves full of diet/health products which again promise instant success if you drink their special formula or eat their special health bar. Watch TV and you'll see the same: numerous adverts for slimming clubs, slimming foods and slimming bars, all with one objective – to help you lose that unwanted weight. We are a nation obsessed with dieting – it's no wonder that so many women in this country have become diet addicts. It is estimated that 90% of British women diet at some point in their lives. Many of these women become calorie-obsessed and caught in a cycle of weight gain, weight loss, weight gain. If you think you might fall into this habit, ask yourself the following:

- Are you calorie-obsessed?
- Do you mentally weigh up every piece of food?
- Do you turn down invitations to go out in case you break your diet?
- Are you always on a diet?
- Do you crave what you'd term 'bad' food?
- Do you look at pictures of food and crave them?

If you've answered 'yes' to any of these you could be on your way to a diet addiction.

Continual restriction of what you eat means that you automatically start to become preoccupied with it. It's human nature, after all, to want something you know you shouldn't have.

Like all eating disorders, diet addiction can and does take over your life. Diets, by definition, divide foods into two categories – good and bad – and hence most people who are on a diet divide themselves into those categories according to what they have or haven't eaten. Many eating disorder specialists now recommend that food shouldn't be emphasized in this way. It's important to stop thinking about calories, diets and weight measurements and start thinking about eating healthily.

The most vital thing to remember is that only 2% of women are genetically likely to have a figure like a supermodel. So if that's what you're striving for in your diet then you're not going to reach it. If you're really sure you need to lose weight (your GP will be able to tell you for sure), then the only healthy way to do it is to eat healthily. This means a diet full of fresh vegetables, lean meat, low-fat produce, fruit and even a little of what you like. This, combined with regular exercise, will help you shed those pounds, slowly but surely.

Forget instant miracle diets and guaranteed weight-loss products; they just don't work for life. When they come off these diets, 95% of women regain all the weight lost in two to three years, and usually sooner.

The so-called miracle diets

Meal replacements

These are powdered soups or milk-shake drinks that provide a low-calorie alternative to ordinary meals. Weight is usually regained after the course ends because the only way you can maintain a healthy weight is by learning how to eat healthily balanced meals.

Crash diets

Apart from being very dangerous to your health, starving your body of food means you are also starving it of vital minerals and nutrients. Crash diets always fail because they throw your body into starvation mode and your metabolism slows down. Therefore, when you do start eating normally again, your body holds on to all the food and you regain all the weight lost and more.

Food combining

Works on the principle that eating acid-forming proteins and starchy carbohydrates at the same time can make you unhealthy and overweight. Nutritionists say that the basic idea behind all this – that the digestive system cannot handle a mix of different food groups – is completely untrue.

Low-protein diets

These diets involve avoiding meat, fish and dairy products and sticking to fruit and vegetables. You lose some weight this way, but your body does need protein to remain healthy and it is dangerous to reduce its supply.

Liquid diets

Highly dangerous and can lead to fainting, dizziness and nausea. Weight is regained as soon as you start eating again.

Too fat

We all have days when we feel too fat and think if only we were thin then everything would be OK. However, if you feel too fat *all* the time, then there are a number of things you can do. The first step is to find out if you really are overweight or not. Don't bother with those silly weight charts, what your friends say or weighing scales. Go to your GP and see whether or not you need to lose weight. If you do, he or she will give you a diet sheet that will help you to eat properly and healthily. This is the safe way to lose weight. Remember, being overweight may not be healthy, but it's better than yo-yo dieting (dieting, then over-eating, then dieting, then over-eating, etc.) and making yourself depressed and miserable for the rest of your life.

If you *are* determined to lose weight, ask yourself why. Is it for health reasons? (If this is the case, then go for it.) Or is it because you think it will improve your life, get you a boyfriend, etc? Sadly, losing weight is not a magical cure for all the things you're unhappy about. Weight gain or loss is just that and nothing else. It doesn't have the power to make your life perfect. Of course, it can improve your self-confidence and therefore make you happier but it won't necessarily make your life wonderful.

If you do decide to diet, then make sure you do it properly and don't crash diet. Crash dieting slows down your metabolism (energy levels) and stops you losing weight. Then when you do start eating again, your body clings on to everything you eat and stores it up as fat and you can't lose weight.

Too thin

Talk to anyone who is thin and you'll hear the same thing: 'No one understands us. They think we're lucky, but we're not.'

Finding it difficult to put on weight is the same as finding it hard to lose weight and for some it's even harder. If you are naturally thin, then exercising could help you a great deal. Muscles can add curves to your body and make you feel better about yourself. If you think you are seriously underweight then don't just stuff your body full of sweets and junk food. It's very important to make sure you eat proper nutritious food to build up your muscles and keep your body and bones strong and healthy.

If you still don't put on any weight then keep a diary of all the food you eat in a week and go along and see your GP, who will tell you for sure if you need to go on a high-calorie diet or not. If you are naturally thin, it doesn't mean you can't be attractive. Don't pin all your hopes on getting a voluptuous figure when the chances of it happening are remote. Be realistic about your body shape: just as most big women will never be waif-like, most thin girls will never be voluptuous.

• Over 24 million fitness videos are sold annually around the world.

• The diet industry in the UK is worth billions of pounds.

• The US diet industry is the fifth largest at $33 billion.

• Ninety per cent of women will diet at some point in their lives – 98% of these will put the weight back on.

• 98% of women see their body as bigger than it actually is.

• 20–30% of women have vomited as a means of losing weight.

• Over 11 million people are dieting at one time.

• 47% of British women are size 16 or over.

• Women are more likely to be underweight than men, yet twice as many women think of themselves as overweight than men.

• Statistics show that plump women live longer than lean or average-weight ones.

EATING DISORDERS

'My friend has such a funny attitude to food. She is quite thin but is always talking about being fat and overweight. She eats hardly anything and works out all the time. Do you think she might be anorexic?'
Fiona (16)

'I am a bulimic and I desperately need your help. I think about food all the time and yet whenever I eat, I end up making myself sick because I can't bear the thought of putting on weight. What can I do?'
Louisa (17)

Eating disorders affect an estimated 70,000 to 200,000 women in the UK alone. There are a number of theories on why this happens; some blame the mother/daughter relationship, others claim it's a fear of growing up and some blame stress. However, what is known is that generally those who have eating disorders are high achievers and perfectionists who have low self-esteem. They never feel they are good enough so they constantly strive for higher and higher goals. They are also very sensitive and cannot cope with external pressures such as exams, leaving home and family crises. When these occur they may feel so powerless and out of control that they attempt to regain control in the only way they can – through their relationship with food.

If you have an eating disorder, it is extremely difficult to acknowledge that you need help, and being forced to eat by other people is not a solution. Help comes in various forms and from various people. If you want to seek help, ask your GP. Alternatively, the Eating Disorders Association (see 'Resources') offer help and advice to sufferers and their family and friends.

Anorexia

Teenage girls need to consume at least 2,000 calories a day in order to sustain the necessary changes the body undergoes during puberty. Very low-calorie diets interfere with this process and can stop your growth altogether. If you are starving yourself or eating less than 1,000 calories a day (one meal a day) then you are starving your body of energy, nutrients and vital vitamins and minerals. Physical symptoms will include fainting, nausea, depression, bad skin, tiredness and lethargy.

Anorexia nervosa is a disease which is about more than excessive dieting. The sufferer can starve herself to death without realizing that she is actually thin. In her mind she is always fat. Sufferers may also embark upon vigorous exercise regimes and weigh themselves several times a day – their whole lives become centred around food and weight. Anorexia is a destructive way of trying to deal with problems, and a way of trying to control a life you don't understand. It is in fact a cry for help, and it is professional help that the sufferer needs. If you think you are anorexic, or if you know someone who needs help, then contact the Eating Disorders Association (see 'Resources').

Bulimia

Bulimia is an eating disorder which is as fatal as anorexia, but unlike anorexia it can often go unnoticed because a bulimic person can look as if they are maintaining a healthy weight. It is also known as the binge/purge syndrome. This means that bulimics eat masses, then make themselves sick, in order to control their weight. Some girls don't eat for days, then consume huge amounts of food in a very short time, only to vomit it all up. Abuses of laxatives and diuretics are other methods bulimics use to try and control their weight.

Like anorexia, this disorder will destroy both your health and your state of mind. If you think you have this disorder, you need to get help to control it before it starts to control you. Contact the Eating Disorders Association or your GP.

Compulsive eating

Any eating disorder is an expression of a deep emotional conflict and compulsive eating is no different. Contrary to what some people may think, compulsive eaters are not greedy. People who suffer from this may be overweight or they may look slim or even thin. Compulsive eaters feel unable to regulate their food intake; for them the mere thought of food is a continuous nightmare. They feel powerless when faced with food, and eat more when they feel depressed, upset, angry or anxious. At these times any food can and will be eaten regardless of the time of day or how hungry the person is. Sometimes compulsive eating may be accompanied by self-induced vomiting and followed by severe dieting. It is important to remember that compulsive eating, like any eating disorder, is a cry for help and that there are people who can help you overcome it (see page 94).

Medical consequences of eating disorders

- Loss of periods.
- Fainting, dizziness, depression and insomnia.
- Heart, kidney and stomach damage.
- Panic attacks.
- Excess body hair.
- Tooth decay.
- Bowel damage.
- Increased chance of self-harm (cutting oneself) and suicide attempts.

Signs to watch out for

It can be hard to be a friend/sister/brother/parent of someone suffering from an eating disorder because you'll undoubtedly feel helpless and angry and at the same time want to help. You may not be able to help the sufferer overcome her disorder but you can help by not covering up for her. Also important are listening and accepting that the sufferer's character changes are part of the illness. If you suspect someone you know has an eating disorder, watch out for the following signs:

- Skipping meals.
- Lying about what they eat.

- Dramatic weight gain or loss.
- Obsessive exercising.
- Going to the bathroom directly after each meal.

Remember, eating disorders always get worse if they are not treated. Treatment is based around resolving underlying problems and may involve family therapy.

Further information
For help and information on eating disorders, contact the Eating Disorders Association, the Maisner Centre or Diet Breakers (see 'Resources').

PLASTIC SURGERY

'I desperately want to have some plastic surgery on my face. My nose is too big, my ears stick out and I hate myself. I saw a TV programme where a woman had her whole face done and she looked fantastic. Can I go to my doctor and get this free on the NHS?'
Lorna (15)

Plastic surgery has become more and more popular thanks to the abundance of people in the public eye who openly talk about the wonders of 'going under the knife'. Every year 60,000 people in the UK pay out for cosmetic surgery in the hope that it will make them more attractive and maybe even beautiful. The surgery itself can be painful, scarring and sometimes even a failure, but this doesn't stop people from going through with the operations.

Plastic surgery has worked wonders for people whose lives have been severely affected by a 'defect' or a 'flaw'. It has also worked near-miracles on people who have been severely burned or hurt in an accident. This doesn't mean plastic surgery is just for people with serious injuries – sometimes a person may have a 'flaw' they just can't live with (e.g. a crooked nose) and this flaw may affect them so much that surgery is the only answer.

However, it's important to realize that though plastic surgery may help you to look better, it won't help you to feel better. Many people have gone through operations which they thought would suddenly make their lives wonderful only to emerge with a new nose or new breasts and the same old attitude about themselves. Before you consider going through any kind of cosmetic surgery it may be worthwhile to examine your self-esteem and also to look at how real your expectations of the operation are. If you are realistic about what a new nose or new breasts, etc. can do for your life, you won't be disappointed.

The other problem with plastic surgery is that it is very expensive. Unless you have a medical reason or have been in an accident, it is unlikely that you will get the operation free on the NHS. This means paying at least £1,000. If you still want to go ahead, make sure you go to a reputable surgeon. Your GP should be able to give you details of where to go, or you could contact the British Association of Aesthetic Plastic Surgeons (see 'Resources').

Rhinoplasty (nose operations)

The nose is the one area that can be changed dramatically without scarring. Though this operation can be performed on young people, most surgeons prefer to wait until the bone growth in the nose is complete. So you'll have to wait until you are around 16 or 17 years old. The operation is done by removing or altering the bone or cartilage in the nose. The skin over the top is then remoulded to change the shape of the nose. All this is done from the inside of the nose so as not to leave scars. After the operation be prepared for lots of swelling and black eyes. The bruising goes after about three weeks, but it can take up to six months for all the swelling to die down.

Breast implants

This surgery is not usually performed before the age of 20 because this is when breast development is usually complete. It is performed by inserting a soft bag of silastic gel (silicone) into a small incision below the breast. The bag is placed under the breast tissue over the chest muscle. It is possible to go up three cup sizes with this operation. After the operation the breast will feel tight and uncomfortable as breast tissue forms around the implant. A support bra must be worn for the next six weeks. Most doctors recommend no stretching or lifting for a further month. The scarring (if any) is hidden by the fold of the breast.

Breast reductions

This is a much more common operation in the UK, as lots of women undergo it in order to relieve back pain. It is a much bigger operation and the scarring is much more obvious afterwards; even though the scar will fade it will not go away. The operation is done by removing excess skin and breast tissue via an anchor-shaped incision that goes around each nipple and down and under each breast. After the operation the bandages have to stay on for up to two weeks and the patient has to be careful for a further two months.

Liposuction/Liposculpture

Liposuction removes fat tissue from the body. It works by making a small incision in the skin and inserting a metal tube into that incision. This tube is connected to a vacuum pump and the fat is literally sucked out. Liposculpture uses a fine needle and a hand-held syringe which allows for contouring on smaller areas.

There are a number of drawbacks to these techniques: they are not a substitute for dieting and exercise, and they cannot be performed on overweight people. They are also very painful and bruising can last for at least a month. There is also a concern about how safe these techniques are, as nerve damage has been reported.

Otoplasty (ear operations)

This is one of the most simple cosmetic surgery operations. The skin of the ear is partially separated from the stiff cartilage that holds the ear to the head. Then some of the cartilage is removed, and the ear is repositioned and stitched into place. All this happens behind the ear, so there are no visible scars. The swelling takes about two weeks to subside.

Chapter Five

HEALTHY LOOKS

The beauty industry is big business all over the world. Look in any chemist and you'll find hundreds of products promising you everything. Healthy shiny hair, beautiful white teeth, a contoured body and perfect nails are all there for a small fee. However, you can have all these things for practically nothing by learning to look after your body.

Regular exercise, healthy eating and common sense will do more than save you money. They will actually make you feel better, look better and age less quickly. Don't be like the other people who ruin their natural good looks and then spend the rest of their life regretting it. Look after what you were born with and it won't let you down for the rest of your life.

EXERCISE

Nothing is better for you than regular exercise. Studies show that 20 minutes of aerobic exercise three times a week increases your fitness. It decreases stress, helps keep depression away, prevents sleeplessness and increases your all-round energy. Not all exercise gives you the same kind of fitness, but strength (muscular endurance like working with weights), flexibility (stretching and body conditioning) and aerobic exercise (burns fat and builds up the heart, lung and circulation capacity) can all be achieved through swimming, for example.

Don't be put off exercise just because you hate PE at school. If you do a sport you like, it can become fun and it will be of great benefit to you in the long run. Try to find something that suits you. Check out your local sports centre and/or work out on your own.

Exercise tips

- For all-round fitness do a mixture of activities that work your muscles, flexibility and aerobic capacity.
- Walking is excellent exercise. Studies have shown that walking a mile a day reduces the risk of osteoporosis (brittle bones) in later life.
- Roller-skating is brilliant for aerobic fitness, strength and flexibility.
- Dancing is good for all of the above too.
- Climbing stairs is good for aerobic exercise.

If you are interested in a particular sport and don't know how to get involved, contact the Sports Council (see 'Resources').

SKIN

Our skin protects us from all kinds of things; it acts as a barrier, protecting our internal organs from damage and guarding against bacteria entering the body. The top layer of the skin is called the epidermis; it is made up of cells that are in the process of dying and renewing themselves. The layer below is known as the dermis; this contains the hair follicles, oil glands, nerve endings

and blood vessels. The last layer is called the hypo-
dermis, and this is where the fat cells, muscles, and
veins are.

The skin, like many parts of our outer body, reflects
how healthy we actually are. If we neglect ourselves,
smoke, drink, deprive ourselves of sleep, forget to take
our make-up off, etc. then it will show up in our skin.
So learn to look after it and you'll literally glow with
health.

Tips for healthy skin

- Drink lots of water – it stops your skin dehydrat-
  ing. No matter how much water we apply externally, the skin still gets most of its water from
  inside. Up to 90% of the water our bodies use is
  absorbed from our food and drink via the colon.
  Doctors recommend that we drink at least a litre
  of water a day.
- Don't smoke – it robs your skin of oxygen and
  dehydrates it (as well as increasing your chances
  of dying of lung cancer).
- Laugh a lot. Children laugh and smile on average
  400 times a day, an adult only 15! Laughter is
  good for you – it speeds up your heart and boosts
  your circulation and oxygen intake. It also leaves
  your nerves and muscles relaxed.
- Exercise boosts the metabolism and maintains
  natural cell health.
- Stay out of the sun. 90% of visible ageing marks
  are caused by the sun.
- Don't scrub your skin – cleansing daily is more
  than enough.

- The skin is the largest organ of the human body.
- It accounts for 16% of total body weight.
- 90% of household dust is dead skin cells.
- 70% of teenagers get acne.

Birthmarks

'I was born with a big birthmark on the left side of my neck that reaches up to my face. I hate it because it is so noticeable. How did I get it and what can I do about it?'
Donna (15)

Few people are born with perfect, blemish-free skin. Most babies have the odd pressure mark or bruise caused by the birth process. Most of these marks disappear within a few days of birth, but some don't. No one quite knows why birthmarks occur but one thing is certain: they are not linked to what the mother did, ate or drank during pregnancy.

The most common birthmark is called the pigmented naevus. This is a large mole of light or dark brown colouring. It can either be flat or slightly raised. Sometimes the mark is a few inches across, other times larger. The colour comes from the natural skin pigment melanin, which for some reason has been programmed to produce extra pigment in a particular area of skin.

Perhaps the most obvious birthmarks are the port wine stain and the strawberry naevus. They have nothing to do with melanin as the colour comes from abnormal blood vessels. The strawberry naevus begins as a tiny red spot that grows and turns a deep red; later the area becomes peppered with tiny white dots (like a strawberry). The white dots are actually patches of normal skin that enlarge and join up until the patch turns the same colour as the rest of the skin and the birthmark disappears.

The port wine stain is a larger area with a purple/ red colour and is the result of malformed blood vessels in the skin. Unlike the strawberry naevus it won't disappear, but it also won't grow bigger or spread.

Port wine stains can't be helped by plastic surgery because the blood vessels' abnormality runs too deep. However, there are a number of special make-ups available which can completely cover up birthmarks. These products are usually available at large branches of Boots or can be obtained on prescription from your doctor. One such make-up is called Keromask; it is waterproof and adaptable to all skin colours. For more information on what to do about birthmarks contact your GP.

Cysts

'I have just been told I have a cyst above my eye that has to be removed. Is it cancerous?'
Helen (17)

Cysts aren't cancerous and they can develop anywhere in the body. They form just below the skin and are filled with liquid. They are harmless but it's always a good idea to see your doctor about any lumps or bumps that appear. He or she can tell you exactly what a particular lump is, and if it is a cyst will usually remove it. This is to stop it getting bigger. The technique is simple: the doctor will either cut the cyst off (under local anaesthetic) or drain it with a type of syringe.

Warts

'I have warts all over my hands. It seems I just get rid of one and another appears. They are so ugly and gross. What can I do about them?
Tina (16)

About 10% of teenagers have warts. They are caused by a virus and are highly contagious. They are spread from hand to face (and vice versa), from hand to hand and from face to face. Most disappear within a year. There are several different types of warts:

- Common warts – flesh-coloured lumps less than a centimetre across.
- Flat warts – flat-topped, flesh-coloured and sometimes itchy.
- Digitates – dark coloured growths.
- Filiforms – long slender growths which usually occur on the eye lids, armpits and neck area.

Warts can be treated by using liquid nitrogen; they can be cut away by your GP or burnt away with chemical paint. For more information see your GP or your local pharmacist.

Another kind of wart is found on the soles of your

feet, and is called a verruca. See page 124 for more details.

Moles

'What are moles and how come I've got them? I have heard they are related to skin cancer – does this mean I am going to get skin cancer?'
Fiona (16)

Moles appear in childhood and we usually have our full quota (around 10–20) by age 13–16. They begin as flat brown spots, become raised and then fade. They occur in an area of the skin where there is a heavy amount of the skin's natural pigment, melanin. Moles can vary in colour and sometimes they can be hairy. Never pluck or shave hairs protruding from a mole, as this leaves it open to bacteria and possible infection.

Moles are harmless and can be removed, but the removal will leave scars. One mole in a million turns into melanoma (skin cancer). This type of cancer is nearly always caused by sun damage. However, if you have a mole that suddenly changes colour, grows, bleeds, itches or hurts see your doctor.

Skin cancer – Melanoma

'I am really fair with red hair and I am always being warned about being careful in the sun. How can I protect myself against skin cancer. Is a sunscreen enough?'
Sue (17)

Malignant melanoma is cancer of the pigment cells of the skin. There are various types of this kind of cancer but the most common is a mole which starts to enlarge and grow. It may change in colour or grow in an odd shape. Melanomas are usually flat, but they can also bleed, itch and become lumpy. The skin surrounding them can also become inflamed.

Melanoma is caused by exposure to ultraviolet light, through strong sunlight or sunbeds. If it is detected early on and the mole is removed, the cancer has a good chance of being stopped. But if you do nothing about it and it starts to affect deeper tissues, there is a high risk of it getting into the bloodstream and spreading to your organs.

The people who are most at risk are fair-haired and red-headed people; also people with freckles and people who expose themselves to the sun (no matter what their skin colour) with no protection. People with a lot of moles may also be at risk if they don't take care.

Sun care

People who live in hot countries know how to behave in the sun (sadly most people from the UK don't). They know that you can't lie out in the midday sun even with protection on. They know that fair skin burns more easily and that the sun ages and wrinkles skin. When on holiday, it's important to build up the time you spend in the sun; the worst possible thing you can do is throw yourself into the sun for eight hours on the first day of your holiday.

Ultraviolet sunlight rays are responsible for skin

damage. These ultraviolet rays are divided into two types: UVA (longer tanning rays) and UVB (shorter burning rays). Both occur on sunny days, but UVBs are also present on cloudy days in summer. If you are going out in the sun, it's important to protect yourself in the following ways:

- Wear the right sun protection cream. Studies now show that in very hot sunlight anything below factor 6 is no protection.
- Don't put oil or normal cream on your skin when you're going into the sun – you will burn yourself.
- If you are very fair wear a total sunblock.
- The safest sunscreen for people who are fair or who have ever burnt themselves is factor 15.
- If you are fair-skinned, do realize that you will not tan no matter how long you stay in the sun.
- Wear sunblock all the time, or keep to the shade. Sudden bursts of intense sunlight can damage your skin, as UVB rays are stronger than UVA rays.
- Don't sit out at midday. Stay inside from midday to three o'clock.
- Protect your head by wearing a hat.
- Be careful in the water or on the sand, since both reflect and intensify sunlight on to your skin.
- Make sure your sunscreen protects you from UVA and UVB.
- Sunbeds produce mainly UVA light which is less dangerous than natural light, but they will damage the skin if used regularly.
- If you do get severe sunburn see your doctor.
- Remember even on non-sunny days you can get

burnt (by UVB rays), so always use a sunscreen when you're out.

• Women spend £11 million per year on after-sun products.

Stretch marks

'I put on quite a lot of weight last year and now I have this disgusting track marks across my stomach and breasts. How can I get rid of them?'
Mary (14)

Stretch marks are breakdowns in the elastic fibres of the skin. They usually occur when the skin has been stretched excessively e.g. during pregnancy, teenage growth spurts and when you put on weight. There is no miracle cure for these red/purple marks but if you keep them well moisturized they will eventually fade and hardly be noticeable.

Spots and acne

'Please tell me once and for all, do chocolate and chips cause spots? I've heard they do but some of my friends (who aren't spotty like me) eat them and they don't have spots.'
Lisa (14)

'I have been told I have acne but I'm not sure what this is. All I know is that it is ugly and lumpy and it hurts.

It's also on my back and starting to appear on my chest. Help!'
Celia (15)

Spots have nothing to do with how clean or unclean you are. And happily for most people research now shows that spots aren't caused by chocolate, sweets or chips. Most spots, especially red, lumpy ones, are caused by the hormone testosterone. This is why they appear just before you get your periods and at times of stress.

Acne happens during puberty, when your sebaceous glands (where oil is produced) are activated by the hormone testosterone. They become enlarged, especially on the face, back and chest and start producing an oily substance (sebum) needed to lubricate the skin. When the sebum overproduces it plugs up the gland outlet – the skin pore. The pore then becomes inflamed and the result is a blackhead. The build-up of oil in the pore is then broken down by bacteria, these penetrate into the skin and a swelling occurs, closely followed by pus cells entering the area.

If the spot is left alone it will eventually rupture and settle down. If the spot is squeezed too early the pus will rupture on to the skin and cause even more swelling.

The good news is that acne eventually clears up of its own accord but in the meantime you can help yourself by not picking your spots. Picking at them makes them bigger, leaves scars and spreads them. Also, tempting as it is, don't waste your money on miracle spot products – they are only a temporary solution and can actually make your skin worse by drying it up and stripping it of its natural oils.

If you have acne your best bet is to see your GP. Acne is a medical condition and your doctor can give you the right antibiotics to fight it. The treatment often takes up to six months to work but it's well worth it in the end, so don't give up on it.

For further information contact the Acne Support Group (see 'Resources').

Perspiration

Sweating is a normal bodily function. It is our bodies' natural cooling-down system and regulates body temperature. Perspiration under the arms is normal, but during puberty and around our periods our sweat glands can overproduce and may cause excessive sweating.

However, body odour is another matter entirely. Sweat doesn't actually smell until it comes into contact with the air and bacteria. Once it dries on clothes it smells sour and stale, and if you don't wash and change your clothes, you'll smell too. You can beat it by making sure you wash at least once a day, using an antiperspirant (not deodorant which is just a perfume spray) and wearing clean clothes every day. Cotton clothes help reduce sweaty smells while man-made products such as viscose and nylon encourage them.

SLEEP AND INSOMNIA

'I can't sleep at night. I seem to lie awake for hours and then feel all panicky and restless because I know I'm going to be tired again in the morning.'
Anne (15)

'How much sleep is a person supposed to have? I seem to only need six hours but my mum doesn't believe me. She says eight hours is what everyone needs.'
Allie (14)

The old 'eight hours a night' is a myth: everyone's body clocks are different and some people need more sleep than others. 66% of us need between 6.5 and 8.5 hours, 16% need more than 8 hours and 18% need only 6 or under. A good test to see if you're getting the right amount of sleep is to test how long it takes you to fall asleep. Well-rested people need only 13 to 17 minutes to fall asleep.

A good way of maintaining general health is to make sure you have a regular sleeping pattern. Getting up and going to bed at regular times every day is better for your health than getting up early during the week and sleeping late at weekends. Don't be tempted to lie in at weekends as you'll wake up feeling sluggish. This is because your brain will get confused and you'll go into a state of sleep inertia – very like jet lag.

Studies in the USA show that hormone levels vary when sleep levels are disturbed, which may be why we get acne flare-ups and dry skin when we can't sleep at nights.

Bags or dark patches around the eyes occur because

when we are sleep-deprived our circulation changes. The body struggles to fight tiredness and blood is diverted to major organs, draining the face of colour and highlighting colour under our eyes.

Some people can't sleep because they are too stressed and restless to relax into sleep. If this sounds like you then some relaxation techniques or listening to soothing music can help to calm you down. Here are some other tips to help you get a good night's rest.

- Thirty minutes of exercise a day helps you to sleep better at night.
- Don't drink tea, coffee or fizzy drinks before you go to bed; caffeine will keep you awake.
- Keep a window or door open. Stuffy rooms can keep you awake.
- Don't eat a heavy meal after 8 p.m.
- Don't go to bed until you are tired.
- If you are still awake after 30 minutes, get up and do something until you get sleepy.
- Don't sleep during the day.
- Try getting up earlier. This may help because the time we are awake is directly related to how long it takes us to fall asleep. The longer we've been awake the quicker we'll fall asleep.
- Keep regular waking-up times. Trying to catch up at weekends means you won't sleep well on Sunday night and the pattern will start all over again.
- Don't panic if you can't sleep. The more stressed-out you get, the harder it will be to sleep. If you find your anxiety rising take deep breaths and try to clear your mind.

- 66% of people sleep for between 6.5 and 8.5 hours a night.
- 16% of people sleep for more than nine hours.
- We dream for about 90 minutes a night.

HAIR

Like your skin, hair is a natural indicator of how healthy you are. To maintain healthy hair make sure you have it cut regularly, especially if you're prone to split ends. If you dye, crimp, or use any kind of heating product on your hair make sure you use a conditioner to keep your hair protected, and always follow the instructions carefully. Hairdryers should not be held close to hair; keep them 6 to 8 inches away from your head. If your hair looks dull it could well be due to a build-up of hair products such as shampoo residue, mousse, gel and hair spray. Rinsing your hair properly after washing can help restore the shine, as can a healthy diet full of protein.

Don't worry about hair loss; it's normal to lose a certain amount of hair, especially if you have fine hair. However, if you suddenly lose a great deal of hair or find yourself with intense itching on your scalp you need to see your GP.

Dandruff

No one is quite sure what causes dandruff but it is thought to be caused by an overgrowth of a fungus that is normally found on the scalp. It appears as scales of dead skin which are shed from the scalp in white flakes. A number of medicated shampoos (available from your local chemist) can help with this condition. It's sometimes a good idea to see your GP if your dandruff is very bad as he or she can prescribe a special medicated shampoo.

Lice

Also known as nits, head lice are tiny insects which cling to hair shafts. They can be caught by anyone as they are passed from head to head and they prefer clean hair to dirty hair. The lice reproduce by attaching their eggs to the base of the hair. The first indication that you have caught lice will be intense itching on your scalp that can't be relieved by scratching. Lice are treated by using a shampoo which contains a safe insecticide; see your GP or pharmacist.

- In Britain we use 21,000 tonnes of shampoo annually.
- Bad-hair days for girls could well be due to hormonal changes in oestrogen and testosterone.
- There are approximately 100,000 hairs on the scalp alone.

Excess body hair

Body hair is a personal subject. Most girls prefer to get rid of it as they feel it is unsexy and unclean to let it grow. Whatever you choose to do is up to you. In terms of health, as long as you wash every day and wear clean, well-ventilated clothes your body hair won't be a problem. Many girls like to remove bikini line hair (hair which follows the line to the top of your thigh), as it can show when you wear a swimsuit.

If you do want to get rid of your body hair, beware: once you start, you will have to keep it up at regular intervals (except electrolysis).

Shaving

Never shave facial hair, because you'll end up with stubble. Use a depilatory cream instead. As for your bikini line, shaving is not recommended here as stubble in this area is often more unsightly (and more uncomfortable) than hair. Instead, try waxing or depilatory creams. When shaving your legs (or armpits), it's important to remember three things:

- Always use a fresh, clean razor (stealing your brother's or your Dad's is unhygienic and will blunt the blade, causing them to get nicks on their face when they shave).
- Never dry shave. Always use water and soap or shaving foam before you shave.
- Always shave in the direction the hair grows; this will stop ingrowing hairs (hairs which when growing curl back into the follicle, causing nasty infectious bumps) and keep your legs smoother.

Depilatory creams

Excess hair, particularly on the face, can be an embarrassing problem for some girls. If you feel you have facial hair you can't live with, you could use a depilatory cream (available from a good chemist) to get rid of it. These creams work by dissolving the hair but do not remove the hair permanently. Follow the instructions carefully and make sure you do a patch test before you try it out on a larger area. IMPORTANT: Depilatory creams are not meant for the whole of your face and should only be used on a moustache, not on your cheeks. Creams can also be used on underarms, bikini lines and legs, but can prove expensive to do regularly. Many smell very off-putting, but some are specially 'fragrance-free'.

Bleaching

Cream bleaches for use on face, legs, arms can be bought from any chemist. Again you have to be very careful with them and do a patch test first. It's also a good idea to try a small area first just to see if you like the results. For some girls with darker skin, having blond hair on their face is just as obvious as dark hair.

Waxing

Perhaps the most common areas to be waxed are the legs and the bikini line. The hair on the legs needs to have at least three to four weeks' growth before it can be waxed. Prepare yourself for a certain amount of pain. Hot (not boiling) wax is spread on an area and special material is applied over it and quickly ripped off, taking the hair with it. This method is not permanent but it lasts a lot longer than shaving or depilatory creams.

You can remove bikini line hair yourself with waxing strips bought from any chemist, but it is quicker and less painful if you have it done at a beauty salon.

Electrolysis

This is a very expensive, painful but permanent method of removing hair. Tiny electrodes are placed through a needle into the hair follicle and a small electric current is passed through which destroys the hair at the root.

If you want to use this method make sure you go to a recognized professional beauty therapist. *Do not* use a home electrolysis kit.

- 66% of women remove body hair.
- 84% of all 12–16 year-old girls remove body hair.
- Women spend £20 million per year on depilatory creams.

MOUTH AND TEETH

Like hair and skin, your dental health is an important sign of overall health. If you have bad breath, tooth decay and bleeding gums the chances are your health isn't that great.

Teeth

In order to make sure your teeth stay healthy you should visit the dentist every six months. The dentist will examine your teeth and gums and answer any questions you might have on dental health. The hygienist is a specially trained member of the dental team who will clean your teeth and let you know how you can keep them clean and healthy.

To maintain healthy, strong teeth you should brush your teeth at least once a day using a medium-textured, nylon-bristled toothbrush. Dentists recommend you change your toothbrush every three months, and brush each day for at least three minutes. Use a toothpaste with fluoride, as fluoride is naturally absorbed into the tooth enamel making your teeth more resistant to decay. Dental floss is a waxed thread which is used to clean between teeth and reduce the risk of gum disease.

Tooth decay and gum disease are caused by plaque (a coating of bacteria which lives on teeth and gums). Plaque occurs when bacteria turn any sugar we eat into acid. This acid starts dissolving the enamel on the outside of our teeth. If you eat too much sugar and don't brush your teeth, cavities (holes that need filling) will develop.

If allowed to remain on the teeth, plaque may harden and form a deposit called calculus (tartar). This can then cause gum disease (gingivitis) which inflames the gums. If this is not treated it can turn into periodontitis which can cause your gums to recede and your teeth to loosen and maybe fall out. This can be prevented by regular flossing and brushing.

Teeth and headaches

The way your teeth meet together (occlusion) can cause problems. If you clench or grind your teeth, or get bad headaches, neck and shoulder pain or discomfort on the side of your face – you have occlusal problems and should see your dentist.

Registering with a dentist

Your local Family Health Services Authority will have a list of all dentists registered under the NHS in your area. NHS dental treatment is free for teenagers up to their 18th birthday, for students in full-time education up to their 19th birthday, for people on low incomes and for pregnant women. For further information write with an s.a.e. to the British Dental Health Foundation (see 'Resources').

Bad breath

Lots of people have bad breath without even knowing they do. This is because you usually can't smell it until it is very bad. If you're not sure, check to see if your tongue is always coated or if you constantly have a sour taste in your mouth. There are a number of reasons for bad breath – tooth decay, indigestion or a gum infection.

Most bad breath is caused by teeth problems and this is why it's important to see your dentist regularly. In between visits make sure you brush and floss your teeth regularly. Some dentists recommend doing this after every meal but twice a day should be enough. Drinking lots of water is also very important because this will thoroughly flush your whole digestive system out.

Another cause of bad breath is diet. Make sure you

have a healthy diet with lots of fresh vegetables and not many refined foods like sweets and fizzy drinks. Eating heavily spiced foods or very rich food is also more likely to make your breath smell.

If you try all this and your breath still smells, visit your GP as your bad breath may have more to do with a gastric problem.

Cold sores

Cold sores are the ulcer-like bumps that form on the lips or around the nostrils. They are caused by the herpes simplex virus type I. Never kiss a person who has a cold sore as the virus may spread to you, and if you have one be careful not to kiss anyone either.

The herpes simplex virus (or cold sores) is highly contagious because during an attack the virus is present on the surface of the skin and also in saliva. Once the virus is in your body it lies dormant until the moment your immune system is weakened by illness and it is reactivated.

Sudden climate changes like strong sunlight or ultraviolet light from sunbeds, emotional stress and tiredness, menstruation and illness such as a cold can also trigger a cold sore. Remember, if you're prone to cold sores, use a lip screen of factor 15 or more while in the sun.

The first signs of a cold sore are a tingling, burning sensation in the area where the sore will develop. In the next stage, the area will become inflamed and red blisters will form on the skin. The blisters will then burst and join up to form ulcers and this is the most painful stage. The healing of a cold sore can then take up to eleven days. Cold sores can be treated by a quick visit to your local pharmacist or GP, where they will prescribe an anti-viral cream like Zovirax.

While herpes simplex I is a separate virus from herpes type II (genital herpes) it can be transmitted from the mouth to the genital region, so you should use a condom even when you're having oral sex. If you have genital herpes, go to your nearest genito-urinary clinic (details in your local directory). For further information on herpes, contact the Herpes Association (see 'Resources').

• About one litre of saliva passes through a person's mouth every day.

• We have 5,000 taste buds on our tongues.

NAILS AND FEET

The human foot is made up of 26 bones and 20 muscles. It is very important because it supports the whole weight of your body. There are 22 bones in the hand, which makes it one of the most flexible and sensitive parts of the body.

Nails

'My nails are always flaking off and breaking. They are also peppered with white flecks. What's up with them? Is it calcium deficiency?'
Livvy (15)

The main body of the nail is known as the nail plate and is made up of a protein called keratin. About a fifth of it is hidden under the skin at the base of the nail, which is why you can damage your nails without even realizing it. A person with good health will have nails with a shiny and smooth surface. The plate will appear pink due to the blood supply underneath the nail.

White marks on the nails are signs of nail damage from bumps and bangs rather than indicators of calcium and/or diet deficiency. Diet, however, is important to the texture of the nails. A diet lacking in essential minerals like iron and zinc can lead to brittle and flaky nails. Strong soaps and detergents can also damage the nail and cause flaking and splitting. Nail damage caused by biting, chewing or accidentally tearing the tip of the nail won't damage it permanently. This trauma actually stimulates nail growth as the body speeds up the process to renew this important shield to the fingers.

- About 12% of the world's population are left-handed.
- Nails grow faster in the summer, as sunlight speeds up nail growth.
- The longest ever recorded fingernails belonged to an Indian man whose nails had not been cut since 1952. His thumbnail alone was 48 inches long, and the combined length of all his nails was 205 inches.
- On average nails grow 4 mm per month.

Athlete's foot

'I have itchy feet and flaking skin especially between my toes. Is it athlete's foot?'
Karen (15)

Athlete's foot is a fungal infection, most commonly found between toes. It can be picked up just by walking barefoot across a changing room. The infection usually starts between the little toe and the one next to it and is itchy and sore. Sometimes the skin turns white and soggy before cracking and peeling. If you don't treat it, it will spread to other areas of the foot and even to other parts of the body. It can be treated with surgical spirit to dry out the skin, and with anti-fungal creams. To prevent it, wear cotton socks, dry thoroughly between toes and change your towel regularly. If it persists see your GP.

Corns and calluses

'My feet are in such bad condition. They have corns and are always sore.'
Julia (15)

These develop, usually on the toes, as a result of pressure and/or friction from badly fitting shoes. Always buy shoes that give you the right of amount of space and don't pinch, gape or slip when you walk. If corns persist and become painful see your local chiropodist.

Ingrowing toenails

Cutting your toenails badly will cause the edge to grow into the skin and cause injury and infection to the toe. These must be treated by a doctor. To lessen the risk of ingrowing toenails, always cut your toenails straight across – then use a nail file to shape.

Verrucas

A highly contagious viral wart infection found on the sole of the foot. Unlike most warts, it is not raised but turns inwards and burrows into the skin. It is very painful and is caused by a virus which can be picked up in swimming pools or in the changing rooms at school. Have it treated professionally, especially if it starts to multiply and hurt. See your doctor or a chiropodist.

Manicures and pedicures

It's important to look after your nails but specialists still disagree on whether manicures and pedicures are actually good for them. As long as you're not too rough with your nails then you can keep them in good condition. What's important is always to cut your nails straight across, not from corner to corner. This way you will stop ingrowing nails forming.

For manicures and pedicures make sure you soak your nails first for at least one minute. Then rub off any dead skin with a pumice stone. Next cut your nails straight across and file the edges smooth with an emery board (not a metal nail file). Finally moisturize your hands and feet with body lotion to keep them supple.

EYES

When you're ill your doctor will probably examine your eyes; this is because your eyes can be a window to your health. It's possible for a doctor to spot symptoms of illnesses like diabetes in your eyes. If you get headaches or sore eyes you should get your eyes tested by either an ophthalmologist or an optician, as you could be short-sighted or long-sighted. If you get headaches and you already wear glasses or contact lenses you may need a different prescription.

Contact lenses

There are so many different types of lenses (24-hour disposables, hard, soft, gas-permeable and coloured lenses) that the only way you can decide which is right for you is by trying them out and getting professional advice. Gas-permeable lenses are thought to be among the best because they allow a very high percentage of oxygen to reach your eyes – but they can be uncomfortable. If you decide contact lenses are for you always follow the instructions carefully. Clean them properly (not with tap water or by putting them in your mouth) and don't sleep with them in if you're not supposed to.

Conjunctivitis and styes

Conjunctivitis is an inflammation of the membrane which covers the eye. Its symptoms include redness, pain and discharge. Styes are caused by an infection in the eyelash root that results in a pustule/boil growing at the edge of the lid. Symptoms include red, swollen eyes. Both must be treated by your GP or else they will spread infection and reoccur.

> • Each eye is protected by 200 eyelashes.

Chapter Six

HEALTHY MINDS

Worry, anxiety – they happen to us all and contrary to popular belief they aren't just things that happen once you become an adult. The odd thing about worry is that the initial anxiety may not even be yours. Perhaps you have a father or mother with a drink problem, or parents who fight all the time. Maybe your family has job or money worries that make you feel scared and anxious. Perhaps the pressure is coming from outside the home; you may worry about the future or feel that you can't handle your exams or your friends. All these things add up to one thing – STRESS – and this stress leads to more worry, anxiety and frustration.

Of course we all have ways of dealing with what stresses us out and upsets us. Some of us shout and scream while others cry and hide away. Many try to shake it off by working incredibly hard or exercising to extremes. These are our own personal 'coping mechanisms'; they may not work for anyone else, but up to a point they work very well for us.

But what happens when they don't work any more? What do you do if you just can't get rid of your depression? Or when you can't sleep at night? What do you do when you feel like crying all the time or you hurt yourself on purpose because you feel so desperate? You may lock yourself away or pretend that it just isn't happening, but if you're someone who does those things, you'll know that it just doesn't help. All it does is make the problem worse.

The only thing that helps when you feel this low is to talk to someone. Someone who is good at listening and who will help you to see that there is a way out of your worries. This doesn't even have to be someone you know. An objective outsider such as a counsellor or psychotherapist can be really helpful because they can provide you with a safe and confidential environment where you can talk and find solutions to your worries. If you would like to talk to someone who can offer you these services contact your GP or Youth Access (see 'Resources') and they will be able to refer you. If you don't want to talk to a stranger, perhaps you could talk to an older sibling or an adult you trust.

Don't be surprised if you find it hard to talk at first. It's difficult to discuss the things that hurt, especially when you're afraid that you're doing something 'bad' or 'wrong' or that you're going to be labelled 'mad'. The fact is, as any doctor will tell you, having a healthy mind is just as important as having a healthy body. Without one or both you will not be able to function to your best capabilities.

SELF-HARM

'Sometimes I just can't cope with things. I feel trapped and I find myself doing awful things. I usually use scissors on my arms and scratch at myself until I bleed. Afterwards I feel so guilty and ashamed. I have scars all over my arms and have to wear long sleeves all the time. Why am I doing this?'
Tania (16)

Very little is known about self-harm (self-mutilation, self-injury, cutting oneself). People who know nothing about it view it as a form of attention-seeking; those who have a friend or relative suffering from it see it as a distressing and confusing act. The actual sufferer not only suffers from the distress that leads to self-injury, but also from the mental anguish and humiliation that comes with the knowledge that they are doing something 'abnormal' to themselves.

Self-inflicted injury can include cutting, burning, scratching, picking or gouging at oneself. Doctors now view it as an extreme way of expressing deep distress and frustration. Many young people find themselves under severe pressure from families, school, friends and relationships. Girls often feel pressured to do well at school, be a 'good' daughter, get a boyfriend, and fit in. These external pressures then become internalized when people feel they have no one to confide in and be open with. The feeling of being powerless and worthless then translates into cutting oneself.

So why do women hurt themselves more than men? According to the specialist organization Bristol Crisis Service for Women: 'Women are more likely to repress their anger than men and push their emotions down, leading to depression. Then in self-anger, their feelings are turned inwards and may be released by self-injury.'

Women who practise self-injury are often likely to be bright, intelligent and talented. They appear to outsiders as successful and work hard to keep their secret hidden. Only when the balance tips and they can no longer cope do their actions become apparent to others.

What help is available?

If you are carrying out self-mutilation, the important thing to realize is that it is your coping mechanism for dealing with your stresses and worries. However, with the right kind of help you can find other ways to deal with your problems, ways which don't involve hurting yourself. Your GP can refer you to an experienced psychotherapist or counsellor who can help you to find new ways of coping and help you get to the root of your self harm.

If you give yourself a severe cut you need to seek immediate medical attention. If a cut or burn is infected (the area will become sore, hot and hard and may ooze pus) it is also important to seek medical help.

Remember you have the right to decent medical help and advice. You have the right to have your wounds seen to and the right to seek professional help. Don't deny yourself proper help and advice because you are too worried about what people may think.

Recovering from self-harm is possible only when you learn to deal with the reasons underlying your actions. Understanding your injuries may not be easy. But with the right kind of professional help it is possible.

If you want to make a start on working out why you hurt yourself, ask yourself the following questions:

- When do you hurt yourself?
- How does hurting yourself help you to cope?
- Are there any particular situations that always cause you to attack yourself?
- How do you feel after you've hurt yourself?
- When did you start hurting yourself?

In answering these questions you'll be able to make a start in understanding why you hurt yourself and getting some control over yourself. If you can't face your GP then contact a youth counselling service in your area or contact MIND, who can give you details of local groups.

How you can help someone who hurts themself

The first step in helping someone who self-injures is to realize that there is nothing 'crazy' or 'wrong' about them. As frightening and as terrifying as self-mutilation is, you must try not to be angry about it. Of course, it's natural to be upset if someone you care about attacks themself and it's also natural to want to help them, but losing your temper, issuing ultimatums and threatening them will not help either of you. If anything it will make your friend more secretive and more isolated.

The best way to help a friend who hurts themself is to offer your support and understanding – but don't think you can change them on your own. It's rather like dealing with someone with an addiction: until they decide that *they* want to stop they will not be able to actually stop.

This doesn't mean you have to keep quiet about how you feel. In fact, it can be quite good to let the person know that their behaviour upsets you but also that you understand and want to help. Many people who hurt themselves do so because they feel alone and trapped: listening can help more than you think.

Through all of this it's important to look after yourself. Being close to someone who injures themself is deeply traumatic and distressing and can be quite a burden in your life. Make sure you get the support you need from your friends, parents, and/or a counsellor.

Further information
Contact the Bristol Crisis Service for Women, Youth Access (for details of local youth counselling groups) or MIND (see 'Resources').

STRESS

'I just seemed to get stressed out all the time. Every little thing upsets me and makes me feel unhappy. Everyone says I need to learn to relax, but I can't.'
Caroline (15)

'My parents talk about stress all the time. They blame it for everything, but I don't really know what they're talking about and how I can help them.'
Susan (16)

We are often responsible for our own stress. How can this be? Well, it's simple really – stress occurs when we don't react in the best way to things that happen to us. For instance you may lose your keys or someone may make a mistake that affects you. Instead of looking for your keys or getting the person to rectify their mistake you may fly off the handle, over-react, cry or get angry. People also get stressed by things like exams, pressure at home and peer pressure. An event doesn't even have to be unpleasant for stress to occur; sometimes

Christmas or birthdays can be extremely stressful.

However, stress is not simply something that happens to you, but how you react or cope with outside events that affect your life. In order to learn how to cope with stress you have to change the way in which you deal with the things that happen to you.

'I'm really stressed out because of my exams. The pressure is so intense. How will I learn everything in such a short time? I know I'm going to fail.'
Karen (15)

In her eyes, Karen's stress has come about because of her exams. The reality is that she is stressed out because she didn't cope with the prospect of her exams very well. Instead of learning her work throughout the year she left everything until the last minute and is now panicking and therefore stressed. In order to conquer her stress over exams, she has to learn how to change the way she studies. Of course, stress won't go away overnight, but by starting to make better decisions you can gradually reduce the stress in your life.

Where does stress come from?

Stress is linked to our most basic human response – the 'fight or flight' response. This has always occurred when humans are caught in a threatening situation. The body releases stress chemicals (adrenaline) which cause the heart to beat faster, blood pressure to rise, muscles to tense up and the brain to become alert, ready to either run (flight) or stay (fight). This response should end in some kind of physical activity which uses up the adrenaline, helping us to get back to normal. But in everyday life we rarely have a physical response to our problems because they are usually mental not physical (e.g. fear of failing) and therefore the adrenaline doesn't subside and our bodies stay in a state of over-alertness with high blood pressure and tense muscles.

What damage does stress do?

Stress affects us mentally and physically; it reduces our abilities, makes us tired, irritable and tearful. It can ruin our personal relationships and make us depressed. One of the most common effects of stress is a tension headache. Some people describe this as a tight elastic band around the head, a pain above the eyes and an ache in the neck. If you suffer from this then see your local pharmacist, who can usually give you something to help in the short term.

For more long-term results you will need to learn how to cope more practically with your worries. If it's school work that worries you then talk to your teachers and your parents. If it's peer pressure or boyfriend worries, then learn to talk about your fears with someone you trust, or contact a youth counselling helpline for some free help and advice.

If you are snappy with the people you love or always barking at your friends or relatives it could be because something else is stressing you out. Try and get to the root of the problem by asking yourself what's really bothering you. Is it something your friend did a week ago that you're still pondering on? Is it nothing to do with them at all? Or is it because you're tired because you've got too much work? Highlighting the source of the problem will help you to deal with what's really going on.

The next time someone winds you up and you feel like you're getting stressed out, do the following:

- Breathe slowly.
- Count to 10, and think before you speak.
- Leave the room if things are getting out of hand.
- Work out *why* this person is really annoying you.

Learning to deal with stress

- The first step is asking for help when you feel out of your depth. If you feel you can't cope then say so and ask for help. Struggling on your own is a waste of time, whereas talking about things can really help.
- Exercise is another important factor. Physical activity will use up excess adrenaline and help you to relax your muscles. Exercise also releases endorphins (your body's natural painkillers) into your brain and helps you to feel on a natural high. Exercise will also help you to become physically tired and to relax more easily.
- Teaching yourself to relax can also help. There are various self-help courses available (check your local library) and tapes which you can buy in health shops that can help you to learn how to relax.
- Don't try to be perfect. Be reasonable ab[...] you can and can't achieve; this way yo[...]

always feel like you're failing and that you have to try harder.
- Talk about your worries. Stress build-up has a lot to do with your emotions and worries. If you continually store things up or put them on hold you're asking for trouble.
- Live one day at a time. We're all guilty of worrying about the future and the past. It's the present that matters.
- Cut out smoking, drinking, too much tea and coffee and fizzy sugary drinks: these all add to stress symptoms.
- Learn to say no. This way you'll never be caught in a situation you don't want to be in.

Further information
Contact your GP, the Relaxation for Living Trust, or the MIND Information Department for a list of useful books. (See 'Resources' for addresses.)

Top Ten Teenage Stress-Outs
1. Death of a loved one
2. Divorce in the family
3. Personal injury or illness
4. Relationships
5. Friendships
6. Exams, or school/college ends or begins
7. Change in living conditions
8. Changing schools
9. Christmas and holidays
10. Minor law violation

• Large-scale disasters can lead to many people within one community being affected by Post-Traumatic Stress Disorder (PTSD). On 21 October 1966 in Aberfan, Wales, a waste tip from a coalfield slid down the side of a valley and demolished several houses and a village school, killing 116 children and 28 adults. In 1966 the people of Aberfan were considered to be suffering from 'severe shock'; in 1980 the victims were diagnosed as suffering from PTSD.
• The number of people who suffer from Post-Traumatic Stress Disorder at any one time is equal to about one per cent of the general population.

DEPRESSION

'I am depressed all the time. I wake up and I feel like going back to bed. The day gets worse and by the time I come home from school I just go straight to bed. My mum says I have to snap out of it but I can't. I can't eat, I can't sleep and all I want is to be left alone. Why do I feel like this?'
Anna (16)

Severe depression amongst teenagers is far more common than you might think. There are hundreds of teenagers across the country who feel desperate, and hundreds more who attempt suicide because they can't pluck up the courage to ask for help. MIND, the leading mental health organization, estimates that one in eight teenagers suffer from depression.

People can become depressed for all kinds of reasons; some obvious, some not so obvious. The effects of depression also vary from person to person. For some people their misery is so devastating that normal everyday things become impossible. Others can relate perfectly to everyday things but inside find themselves growing more and more desperate. These people have one thing in common: they believe they have fallen so far that they may never be happy again.

Some of the things you may feel when you're depressed include disliking yourself mentally and physically, hating others, being negative about everything, feeling empty and out of control, feeling guilty, not being able to make decisions, wanting to be alone, fatigue, and irregular sleep and eating patterns.

People who suffer from depression usually experience prolonged unhappiness, isolation, helplessness and despair. Depression can start at any time and if left untreated it can lead to suicidal tendencies. Depression is often accompanied by a wide variety of symptoms and can affect anyone from any walk of life.

Statistics show that at any one time, symptoms of depression will affect between 15 and 20% of the population. Many factors can contribute towards a depression, including psychological factors (such as trauma, bereavement), and social factors (including peer pressure).

If you feel depressed and you just can't deal with daily life, you need to seek help. There is no miracle overnight cure for depression, but learning how to release your pent-up feelings, changing aspects of your life that make you unhappy, and finding ways to look forward to the future are all ways of combating depression.

Learning to talk to friends, family and loved ones is also an important way of learning how to overcome your depression. These people can give you much-needed support and help you to feel less isolated and alone. However, if your depression doesn't go away, a trained and objective outsider such as a counsellor or psychotherapist should be your next port of call. These people are trained to help you overcome your depression and help you find new ways to enjoy life. Despite the popular media image of a 'shrink' or 'quack', seeing a counsellor doesn't mean that you are 'mad', or 'crazy'. It shows that you are tackling your problems head on and not hiding from them. All you have to do is reach out and ask for help. It's hard and it can be painful but it's better than living with no hope.

Prozac

'I keep reading about this miracle happy drug that you get from your doctor. I would like to take it – how can I get it?'
Jules (17)

Prozac is an anti-depressant drug which was licensed in 1987 for the treatment of serious clinical depression. Sadly there is a lot of hype about Prozac which suggests that anyone who is feeling down can take it and be happy. This is not the case. Prozac was designed specifically as a short-term measure to help depressed people get through to the stage where they can start dealing with the problems that are causing their depression. It isn't a miracle cure that can stop depression for ever. The depression comes back the minute you stop taking it if you haven't tried to do anything about the root of your depression in the first place.

If you feel depressed don't think that taking an anti-depressant like Prozac will cure all your problems, because it won't. Tackling your problems head on and talking about them with a trained professional is the way forward.

Suicidal thoughts

'I want to kill myself. I hate my life – nothing ever goes right and there's no point to it any more. It's not a quick decision, I've been thinking of this for a long time.'
Louise (16)

There is no problem that can't be worked out as long as you ask for help. This is why suicide is never your only option. If you feel at all suicidal or even just go through phases when you ponder on it, please seek help. The Samaritans are on hand 24 hours a day, 365 days a year; and ChildLine are also there to help every day of the year (see 'Resources'). Alternatively, your GP can refer you to someone who can help. Talking through your problems with someone who under-stands is more helpful than you think. All worries are things that can be worked through. They are not things for which you throw away your life.

If you have a friend who talks about killing themself,

take them seriously. Signs to watch out for are: severe depression, sudden manic behaviour, withdrawal from friends and family, and the giving away of possessions. Make sure you show your friend that you care and you want to help. Encourage them to seek help and to tell an adult (parent, teacher, counsellor) what is going on.

Further information
The following will provide help and more information on depression. (See 'Resources' for addresses.)

- Your GP.
- Fellowship of Depressives.
- ChildLine.
- The Samaritans.
- Depression Alliance.
- Defeat Depression Campaign.
- SANE (emergency helpline for relatives and sufferers from mental illness).
- MIND (National Association for Mental Health – produce an excellent leaflet on depression with more contacts. Send an s.a.e. with a postal order for 45p made payable to MIND.)
- Youth Access (for details of local youth counselling groups).

SEASONAL AFFECTIVE DISORDER

'I've heard so much about a syndrome called SAD but I don't know what it is or how you might catch it.'
Laura (14)

SAD stands for Seasonal Affective Disorder. Symptoms include tiredness, lethargy, depression, increased appetite and mood swings. The condition starts around October when the nights get longer and the days shorter, and continues until March or April.

It is thought SAD is caused by a chemical imbalance in the brain due to shorter daylight hours and lack of sunlight. During winter time, insufficient bright light enters the eye and the body increases production of the sleep-inducing hormone, melatonin. Tests have suggested that SAD sufferers release abnormally high levels of this hormone. This is the hormone that induces hibernation in some animals.

Sufferers can now be treated with light therapy which relieves their symptoms. They need to expose themselves to between two and six hours of very bright light a day. For further information and advice contact your GP or the SAD Association (see 'Resources').

PHOBIAS

'I am terrified of spiders. No one understands how I feel and I know people think I am making it all up. The other day someone put a fake spider on my desk and when I saw it I burst out crying. I felt so stupid but the thought of them terrifies me.'
Jo (15)

A phobia is an irrational but real fear of an object, animal or situation; a terror that is out of proportion to the actual danger involved. Phobics experience severe panic attacks when confronted with their fear. It doesn't even have to be the 'real' object that brings on a panic attack. Sometimes the thought of it, a plastic replica or picture can invoke the fear.

A recent study estimated that there are between five and seven million phobics in Britain. It is thought that most phobias are triggered in childhood; or sometimes a phobia is 'learned' from a family member. Other phobias come in later life; for instance, agoraphobia (fear of leaving your house) can happen when people have been ill for a long time or housebound for whatever reason.

How to beat your phobia

Phobias are treated by a method called *desensitization*. The basic idea behind this is to learn to face your fear head on, instead of running away from it. A trained behavioural therapist will help you do this. In the case of someone afraid of spiders, the phobic will be taught to relearn their ideas about spiders. The therapist may start the phobic off with a picture of a spider, work towards a photograph, then introduce a plastic spider and then gradually work towards dealing with a real one.

This is a very gradual process and no one will make you go near a spider (or your particular fear) if you feel you're not ready. Thousands of people have been cured by this simple technique. Relaxation techniques are also given along the way to cope with anxiety. Contact the Phobics Society (see 'Resources') for further information.

A-Z of Phobias

Animals	Zoophobia
Bees	Apiphobia
Birds	Ornithophobia
Blood	Hermatophobia
Cats	Gatophobia
Confined places	Claustrophobia
Crowds	Ochlophobia
Darkness	Nyctophobia
Death	Necrophobia
Dogs	Cynophobia
Everything	Panphobia
Flying	Aerophobia
Foreigners	Xenophobia
Germs	Spermophobia
Heights	Acrophobia
Injections	Trypanophobia
Insects	Entomophobia
Jealousy	Zelophobia
Knees	Genuphobia
Lightning	Astrapophobia
Mice	Musophobia
Needles	Belonophobia
Open Spaces	Agoraphobia
Pain	Algophobia
Rain	Ombrophobia
School	Scholionophobia
Snakes	Ophidiophobia
Spiders	Arachnophobia
Teeth	Odontophobia
Vomiting	Emetophobia
Wasps	Spheksophobia

PANIC ATTACKS

'I have just been told I suffer from panic attacks but I was too scared to ask what my doctor meant and now I'm really worried.'
Paula (14)

A panic attack is a rapid build-up of anxiety which causes mounting terror in which your heart pounds, you find yourself short of breath, and you feel faint and sick. You may even pass out. The place where the attack happens (e.g. on a crowded bus, in a lift or out on the street) then becomes the trigger for further attacks. The next time the sufferer finds themself in a similar situation, the fear returns, anxiety mounts and another attack can take place.

Sufferers can be helped with a mixture of relaxation techniques and therapy, as with phobias (above). For further information on panic attacks and how to overcome them contact PAX (see 'Resources').

OBSESSIVE COMPULSIVE DISORDERS (OCD)

'I think there is something wrong with my mother. Ever since my father left home she has become obsessed with cleanliness. She washes everything in sight and can't go anywhere without washing her hands all the time. What's wrong with her?'
Jane (14)

Obsessive Compulsive Disorder is a condition in which there are frequent repetitive rituals like washing hands, checking that doors are locked and even dressing in a particular order every day. Sufferers may be unreasonably frightened of dirt, infection, etc. The sufferer feels they have to perform some action such as washing their hands to relieve their mounting tension. OCD usually begins in adolescence or early adulthood; it affects up to 3% of the population.

OCD can be recognized by the following symptoms (the examples relate to a sufferer obsessed with cleanliness):

- Obsessional thoughts (e.g. fears of contamination).
- Obsessional impulses (e.g. to clean everything and so lessen the risk of contamination).
- Obsessional rituals (e.g. persistent cleaning, often with bleach). These actions are senseless and repetitive but it is the only way for sufferers to alleviate their anxiety.

OCD usually follows a period of intense stress. Sufferers are usually highly intelligent. Help can be found through your GP (who can refer you to a behavioural therapist) or through First Steps to Freedom (see 'Resources').

HEADACHES AND MIGRAINES

'I suffer from really terrible headaches. They usually happen when I am at school and when I am studying for exams. I had my eyes checked out because I thought I needed glasses, but I didn't. So what's wrong with me?'
Sarah (14)

There are many different kinds of headaches that happen for many different reasons. Most headaches are triggered by muscular tension; they occur because stress and anxiety cause tension in the muscles around your shoulders and neck. Though painkillers can help, changing your lifestyle is a more permanent way to deal with these headaches. Make sure you have regular sleep, don't skip meals, take up physical exercise and eat healthily. On top of this, try to deal with the stress in your life. What's important, however, is to seek medical help if you suffer from regular headaches.

Hormones can also cause headaches and lots of women get headaches just before their periods. If you are on the pill and find yourself suffering from headaches or migraines, you need to go back to your doctor and tell him what's going on. There are many different kinds of contraceptive pill and you will eventually find one which suits you.

'Now and again I have a terrible headache that lasts for hours. I don't usually suffer from headaches but this one is terrible. I have to lie down and shut the curtains until it goes away. It also makes me feel sick and my eyesight goes funny. I worry that I have a brain tumour.'
Suzanne (15)

Only in incredibly rare instances does a headache signal a brain tumour, though the thought does cross the mind of many people suffering from a stabbing, throbbing headache. Suzanne suffers from what is known as a migraine. This is a pounding headache (usually on one side of the head) that can last for hours or even days. It is accompanied by distorted eyesight, feelings of nausea and sometimes even vomiting. The sufferer may also see flashing lights and weird shapes. Once the headache stage of an attack starts, most people cannot bear bright lights or noise and have to lie in a darkened room. Of course, not everyone who gets migraines will suffer from all these symptoms, and some people will get other symptoms like tingling limbs and perhaps even difficulty in speaking.

It is thought that migraines are caused by temporary changes to the blood vessels around the brain but it is still not known why these changes take place. Unfortunately there is no cure for migraines but you can help alleviate the symptoms by seeing your doctor. He or she can help find the right treatment and tablets to combat your condition.

Apart from drug treatments, help can come from relaxation and finding your particular 'trigger' (the object, situation or stress that causes the attack to come on). Some people find that foods such as cheese, oranges, pork, chocolate and wine are associated with their attacks, and that when they keep away from these they don't get migraines. This is because these foods contain a chemical called tyramine which has been identified as a trigger for migraines.

The next time you get a migraine, note down what you ate just before it and what happened to you; this way you may be able to identify your particular trigger. For further information and help, contact the British Migraine Association (see 'Resources').

Chapter Seven

UNHEALTHY LIVING

People use drink and drugs for all kinds of reasons. Some do it to feel better about themselves, some to escape from their lives, some to fit in with their friends and others because they just can't get through the day without it. Not many of us will go through the whole of our lives without ever trying one or both of these things.

If you haven't yet been tempted to try any of these things I'd like to say, *'Don't do it! They aren't worth bothering with.'* – and leave it at that.

However, we all know it's not that easy. Drink and drugs are tempting for a number of reasons. Apart from the fact that it always looks *fun* to get drunk or 'out of your head', it's also hard to say 'no' when all your friends are doing it. Maybe they make you feel boring and square for not trying things out, or maybe they say it's OK for you to say no, and then act as if it isn't. Perhaps you just don't like being the odd one out. On the other hand, maybe you experiment with drugs so that you can stand out in your crowd. Maybe it makes you feel mature and older. Perhaps you take drink or drugs because it eliminates your shyness and makes you feel confident.

The real problem is, of course, drink and drugs aren't a solution to any of these problems. They won't make you more confident, in fact, they'll have the opposite effect. They'll make you feel that you aren't anything without them and that they are the only way you'll get through life. As for peer pressure, taking substances doesn't prove you're a better friend, only that you're a friend that can't stand up for yourself. Remember, real friends won't encourage you to do something dangerous, they will protect you and stand by you even when you disagree with them.

Letting drink and drugs speak for you will only multiply your problems and worries. They could ruin your health, ruin your life and lose you all your friends. Learning to make realistic decisions now about drink and drugs will help you to give up on them before they take over your life.

SMOKING

'My friends all smoke and I have to admit it looks pretty cool. I want to try it but am worried that I'll become hooked. If I try a couple now and then would it be OK?'
Donna (16)

It looks cool, it appears sexy, and yet it kills! It gives you lung disease, heart disease and cancer, but more young women in the UK are smoking every year. Like drinking and drugs, people smoke for a variety of reasons: to cope with shyness, nervousness and social awkwardness, to appear sophisticated and to fit in.

However, it isn't easy just to have a couple of cigarettes now and then and resist them the rest of the time. The effects of tobacco are immediate and they build up with each cigarette. When a person smokes, their heart speeds up and their blood pressure increases. They will also become addicted to the nicotine in cigarettes very quickly and feel jittery, irritable and depressed if they aren't allowed to smoke. The smoke inhaled will then destroy their circulatory system, and coat their lungs with tar.

Without a doubt smoking is incredibly dangerous. You are 24 times more likely to get lung cancer. You increase the risk of getting heart disease, bronchitis, and ulcers every time you take a puff of smoke. Smoking in pregnancy increases the risk of miscarriage and respiratory problems in babies.

Passive smoking (breathing in other people's cigarette smoke) is also dangerous. The smoke from a cigarette is divided into two kinds: mainstream smoke which is inhaled and exhaled by smokers, and sidestream smoke which is released from a burning cigarette. This sidestream smoke contains ammonia, carbon monoxide and nicotine and can increase the risk of severe breathing problems and cancer in those who inhale it.

As for the myths regarding smoking, it does not help you to lose weight or relax. In fact the nicotine in cigarettes is a stimulant and it speeds up your bodily functions and increases your heart rate. Then, like any stimulant, you will quickly be left feeling irritable, tired and anxious. The carbon monoxide in cigarette smoke also puts extra strain on your heart.

Giving up

Statistics show that six out of ten smokers would like to give up, and I hope that reading the above will make you want to give up too. There are a number of ways you can stop smoking. Some people swear by going 'cold turkey' (i.e. stopping completely), while others find nicotine patches and nicotine chewing gum a perfect way of staving off nicotine cravings.

Stopping a habit isn't easy but with effort you can do it. Try not to say to everyone, 'This is my last cigarette for ever and ever.' Not only is this likely to tempt you back pretty soon but it will also get everyone badgering you. Take each day at a time and remember, just because you slip up and have one cigarette after you've given up doesn't mean you have to dive back in and smoke full time. Take one moment at a time and don't put yourself in situations that will tempt you to smoke. This sometimes means changing your social habits and/or eating habits until you've got it under control.

'I always had a cigarette at lunchtimes in the park with my friends. When I gave up, instead of just sitting about being bored with them I started doing other things like going down to the shops or getting involved with a lunchtime group at school.'
Sue (15)

'I always used to have a cigarette with a cup of coffee. When I gave up it was impossible to have a coffee without craving one so I gave up coffee too.'
Linda (17)

'The three of us always used to sit in the smoking section in McDonald's whenever we all went out because we were all smokers. When two of us gave up we agreed we should sit in non-smoking when we're

'out, so we don't get tempted. So Jane has had to give up too.'
Fran (16)

Remember, giving up will result in an immediate improvement in health. Your breathing and circulation will improve and you will also improve your general health and life expectancy.

Further information
For tips on how to give up and more details, contact ASH (Action on Smoking and Health) or QUIT, the National Society of Non-Smokers. (See 'Resources'.)

- Young people smoke £65 million worth of cigarettes a year.
- 150,000 children leave school each year locked into a habit of smoking that will kill 4,000 of them before the age of 65 years old.
- Smoking-related lung cancer in women has risen by more than 70% in under 15 years.
- Passive smokers have a 10–30% increased risk of lung cancer.
- 40,000 people die from lung cancer each year.
- Smoking currently kills three million people a year worldwide.
- The average twenty-a-day smoker spends £30,000 on cigarettes in their lifetime.
- It is estimated that 44% of household fires are caused by cigarettes.
- Smoking kills over five times as many people in the UK than road and other accidents.

ALCOHOL

'My mother is an alcoholic and I desperately want to help her. She pretends she doesn't have a problem but she drinks all day. By 9 p.m. she's always crying and saying sorry and promising to give up, but she never does. I can't cope with her.'
Alice (15)

'I have always been so shy and ever since I started secondary school it's got worse. Now the only way I can get through a day is by drinking some of my dad's whisky before I go to school and when I come home at lunchtimes.'
Helen (14)

Helping an alcoholic

Alcohol is another of the biggest killers in the UK. 25,000 people die every year as a result of it. And yet it is legal. In fact, 90% of people in the UK use alcohol as part of their social activities. However, if you know someone who turns to alcohol every time something goes wrong or uses it as a way to get through the day, then the chances are they have a problem.

People who drink because it makes them 'feel good' are only fooling themselves. Alcohol is a depressant that slows down the activity of the brain and dulls you to everything. This makes your responses shaky and your judgement dubious. It also pulls you down harder and makes you want to drink more to reach another high. It's a vicious circle that's hard to break out of. Another reason why people who drink can't stop is because it's only a part of their problem. They often drink to hide what's really scaring them.

Until an alcoholic admits they have a problem they won't be able to overcome their addiction. No amount of begging from anyone they know will do them any good or convince them to change their ways. If you live with an alcoholic or know someone suffering from a drink problem you need to seek help, especially if they show no signs of overcoming their addiction.

You need to determine how badly their problem is affecting you and your life. If a parent is drinking, are they putting your life, their life or anyone else's life at risk? If it's a friend/boyfriend/sibling, are they a danger to themselves or to you when they drink? If the answer is yes to any of these problems you need to seek outside help.

Even if you don't feel you are at risk, living with and loving an alcoholic is very hard. Alateen and other organizations (see below) offer help, support and confidential advice to any young person who has to cope with someone's alcohol problem.

Further information

Contact Alateen or Al-Anon Family Groups, organizations which aim to help families of problem drinkers. Alateen deal specifically with teenagers who have been or who are affected by an alcoholic relative. The organizations are completely confidential. See 'Resources' for details.

Effects of alcohol

When we drink alcohol it enters the bloodstream and reaches the brain within five minutes of being swallowed. It remains in the body until it is burnt up by the liver. How we react to alcohol depends on our weight, height, sex and size. A woman will get drunk quicker and on less than a man of the same height. This is because women cannot tolerate as much alcohol as men. Our bodies carry more fat and less water than men's do, therefore the alcohol is more concentrated in our bodies and we will be damaged more easily by it.

Doctors recommend that sensible maximum weekly limits are 21 units for an adult woman (28 for a man), and warn that regularly drinking over three units a day (for women – four for men) can be damaging to health. One unit is equal to a glass of wine, or half a pint of beer or one measure of spirits. Each unit takes your body an hour to burn up. When you drink heavily, apart from giving yourself serious health problems in the future, you will irritate your stomach, causing pain and diarrhoea; you will gain weight, as alcohol contains sugar and carbohydrates; and you will dehydrate yourself and give yourself a nasty headache. You could also hurt yourself badly as your judgement and actions will be impaired by the alcohol.

The most serious thing alcohol will do to your body is damage the liver. If alcohol is present in the blood most of the time, it will prevent the liver from working properly, causing cirrhosis, which can in turn sometimes lead to liver cancer.

Contrary to popular belief, coffee, fresh air, cold water and 'hair of the dog' won't sober you up and/or stave off a hangover. There is no quick way to sober up. It takes our livers a full hour to break down just one glass of wine or a measure of spirits. If you drink a pint of beer it will take two hours. The more you drink, the longer it will take your body to recover. If you want help with a hangover then drink lots of water as that helps with dehydration, always eat something before you drink, and give yourself time to get over it.

If you think your drinking is getting out of control then you need to seek professional help, either through your GP or one of the organizations below. Warning signs to watch out for, in others and in yourself, are:

- Becoming touchy when people talk about your drinking.
- Lying about how much you drink.
- Needing to have alcohol around.
- Drinking alone.
- Using drink to get you through the day.
- 'Binge' drinking on weekends.
- Becoming irritable and anxious if you can't have a drink.

Further information
Your GP can refer you to local agencies where you can go through detoxification (i.e. withdrawing from alcohol) and get relevant counselling. You can also contact Alcoholics Anonymous, Alcohol Concern or Drinkline (see 'Resources').

- In 1950 the average Briton drank 3.7 litres of alcohol a year. By 1990 the figure had doubled to 7.5 litres.
- 77% of girls have their first proper drink by the time they are 13 years old.
- 25% of 13–17 year-olds get into fights after drinking.

- Alcohol has been identified as the largest single common factor in road accidents.
- Alcohol is a major factor in two-thirds of all road deaths at night.
- 25,000 people die every year as a result of alcohol.
- 1,000 children under 15 are admitted to hospital each year with acute alcohol poisoning.
- Women are more sensitive to alcohol, and will become drunk faster and on a smaller quantity just before a period and during ovulation.

DRUGS

'My friends all take drugs, nothing heavy like heroin but things like speed and ecstasy. I've heard they can make life more exciting but I worry about the down side. Should I try it?'
Shannon (16)

The popular media image of a drug user is a young neglected person addicted to heroin or 'off their heads' on ecstasy at a rave. The reality is not quite like that, and with more drugs being available at cheaper rates, you are more likely to come into contact with drugs at a younger age and maybe even at school. Drugs come in all different shapes and forms, and often with names you may never have heard before. For instance, someone may offer you a 'tab' of acid (which is actually LSD) or 'dope' (which is cannabis). To protect yourself from being hurt and/or landing on the wrong side of the law you need to know what's legal and what isn't, and how badly drugs can and will affect you both mentally and physically.

All illegal drugs in this country are divided into three classes: A, B and C. They are categorized according to how dangerous they are, and remember, the higher the class the bigger the penalty if you get caught with them.

- **Class A** drugs are ecstasy, heroin, cocaine, LSD and methadone (heroin substitute).
- **Class B** drugs are cannabis and amphetamines (uppers).
- **Class C** drugs are tranquillizers (which can only be prescribed by a doctor).

If you are caught supplying a drug in Class A, you can face a maximum sentence of life imprisonment as well as a huge fine. However, dealing drugs isn't the only way to get in trouble. Anyone possessing, importing, exporting, and/or supplying drugs is breaking the law. And despite what people may tell you, growing cannabis and magic mushrooms is also illegal.

If you get caught with drugs and you are under 18 years old, the following can happen if you are convicted:

- Under the age of 14, you will be tried in a juvenile court and a sentence will involve restrictions on where you live, what you're allowed to do and what school you can go to. It will also involve counselling.
- Under the age of 18, you are expected to take responsibility for your criminal acts. You could

be sent to a young offenders institution and given counselling.

If this doesn't stop you getting involved with drugs, knowing exactly what they can do to your body will show you why you should say no to them. The first fact to remember is that all drugs can make you dependent upon them but not all can make you addicted.

Being *dependent* on a drug means you use a drug regularly because you rely on its effects (e.g. sedation or stimulation) to help you deal with everyday life. Being without the drug can make you anxious and/or depressed.

An *addiction* involves both the above psychological dependence *and* a physical dependence whereby your body actually needs the drug and can't get by without it. Withdrawal from the drug causes depression, vomiting, nausea, cramps, tremors, panic attacks, etc.

Class A Drugs

Ecstasy
Also known as: 'E', MDMA, XTC, Dennis the Menace, Disco burgers, lovedoves, M25s. Ecstasy is a rave drug with one specific purpose – it stimulates the nervous system and energizes the muscles, which then allows a person to dance for hours and hours. However, it also increases blood pressure and body temperature, which is one of the reasons why there have been a number of deaths associated with E. These deaths have occurred due to respiratory failures, heart failures and brain haemorrhages.

The less fatal pitfalls of this drug include exhaustion, teeth grinding, jaw clenching, anxiety attacks, depression and insomnia. It's important to note that ecstasy is rarely 'pure' these days, and is often mixed with everything from speed to LSD/acid to talcum powder, and ketamine. This means that anything can happen to a user. The worst side effects and experiences occur with those using high doses (i.e. more than one E at a time). These effects include psychosis, panic, confusion, hallucinations and loss of confidence. There is also growing evidence that using ecstasy over a long period of time may cause liver damage in some people.

Ecstasy and dehydration

The most important danger to watch out for is dehydration/heatstroke. This occurs because ecstasy causes the body's temperature to rise. If somebody then dances maniacally for hours and hours, their temperature will rise even more and they will literally sweat buckets. Warning signs of dehydration include stopping sweating, giddiness, cramps, vomiting, needing to urinate and not being able to, and of course, fainting. If you spot someone with these signs, don't give them any alcohol to drink, as this will only dehydrate them further. Take them outside, splash cold water on them to cool them down and then seek urgent medical help.

The best cure for dehydration is prevention, i.e. don't take E. If a friend is insistent on trying ecstasy then at least ensure that they drink water at a rate of about a pint an hour, are wearing cool clothes, and take regular breaks from dancing. If they feel unwell, seek help for them immediately. It is important to keep salt levels up; salty snacks, fruit juice, fizzy drinks and sports drinks all help to keep the body provided with the minerals needed.

Heroin

This can be taken by mouth but works faster by injection straight into the bloodstream. It is also used by heating the heroin powder and inhaling the smoke ('chasing the dragon'). Heroin works by calming the user so that they basically feel nothing. A novice user is likely to suffer unpleasant side effects like vomiting. Opiates (drugs derived from the opium poppy) like heroin are highly addictive and the user has to use higher and higher doses in order for it to have the same effect. When not on the drug the user will feel withdrawal symptoms of anxiety, cramps, fever, sweating and severe muscle spasms. Eventually, even though the user no longer gets any good effects from it, they will continue to do it simply in order not to feel withdrawal symptoms. Heroin addicts also neglect themselves and risk other serious health problems (including AIDS by the use of shared needles) due to the lifestyle they lead as addicts.

Cocaine/Crack

Cocaine usually comes in a white powder form and can be sniffed into the nose. It comes from the leaves of the coca plant grown in South America. It is absorbed quickly through the thin membranes of the nose, and its effects include dilation of the eyes and rising excitement levels. A user will also feel cheerful and energetic. However, cocaine also causes a large amount of anxiety, aggression and paranoia. Frequent use causes insomnia, depression and permanent damage to the membrane of the nose. Repeated use has been known to produce disturbing and irrational fears and anxieties.

Crack is a highly dangerous smokable form of cocaine.

LSD/Acid

Lysergic acid diethylamide is a white powder, but because only small amounts are needed for a trip, it is normally pressed into a small square of paper or gelatine. It is then swallowed and acts after about 30 minutes. Its effects are sensory hallucinations of distorted colour, sound and touch. It might sound all very exciting but taking LSD means risking having a bad trip. This is a hallucination that may be frightening, depressing and scary – a trip from which you can't escape. Some users have become psychologically disturbed after a bad trip. 'Good' trips can be just as dangerous since users can, for example, believe that they are invincible, or that they can fly.

Class B Drugs

Cannabis

Also known as grass, weed, marijuana and pot. Cannabis resin is a soft brownish-black substance that is usually mixed with tobacco and rolled into a 'joint' (cigarette shape). Cannabis tends to make people feel more relaxed and confident. Some people claim it makes them more creative and thoughtful. Others claim it helps them calm down. Some people get no response at all from taking cannabis. Physically it lowers the blood pressure and is not addictive.

It is estimated that four million people in Britain have used cannabis and that half a million use it regularly. Recently, there have been calls to legalize it, as it is less addictive than smoking. It is also said to have effective medical use in the treatment of arthritis, PMS and glaucoma. One of the main dangers of cannabis is the state of intoxication of the user – the person cannot drive or coordinate safely while under its effects. Like tobacco, smoking cannabis can cause respiratory problems.

Uppers/Speed

These are amphetamines, stimulant drugs which come in a tablet or powder form. The tablets are swallowed, and the powder is sniffed. These 'uppers' produce feelings of increased energy and confidence and people find they help them to stay awake for hours and go without food.

Users may find themselves talking and chattering, but will also feel anxious, irritable and may sweat, grind their teeth and become aggressive. Uppers also lead to intense mood swings, violent tantrums and depression. Long-term use leads to heart problems and, because of the loss of appetite, malnourishment and dietary problems. It is also a trigger for mental illness.

Glue-sniffing

Glue-sniffing is also known as solvent abuse; it includes sniffing glue, butane gas, paint, paint thinners and petrol. It is not illegal to sniff solvents but it is against the law in the UK for a shop to sell a solvent to someone they think may inhale its fumes.

People who abuse solvents do so by inhaling them. The solvent is put in a plastic bag and inhaled through the nose and mouth. If an aerosol is used it is sprayed into the mouth.

The result of sniffing is like getting drunk, but it happens faster and wears off faster. As well as feeling drunk, a solvent abuser may get hallucinations which can be terrifying. The dangers of abusing solvents are huge. Not only is there the chance that you may pass out and choke on your own vomit, but aerosols sprayed into the mouth can cause suffocation. Also, the variety of chemicals that get into your body will affect your heart, damage your lungs and liver and destroy your nervous system. You will end up with constant headaches, sores around your mouth and nose and will also suffer from convulsions and depression.

How to tell if someone's on drugs

The following can be symptoms of drug-taking:

- Aggression.
- Loss of appetite.
- Depression and anxiety.
- Need for more money than usual.
- Mood swings.
- Strange sores on the body, or marks on arms (only in some cases).
- Unusual smells, stains on clothes.

Further information
If you or a friend or relative needs help to give up drugs or to cope with someone who is taking drugs, then contact the National Drugs Helpline, SCODA (Standing Conference of Drug Abuse – for details of local drug services in your area), Narcotics Anonymous (self-help group for drug users), Adfam National (helpline supplying help and advice for the family and friends of drug users), or Release (drug information and advice). See 'Resources' for addresses.

- 500 people die every year as a result of illegal drugs.
- In any one year, at least a million people take an illegal drug.
- A recent study found that 28% of 16–19 year-olds had taken an illegal drug.
- Population surveys suggest that 14% of 14–15 year-olds have experimented with drugs.
- There were 28,000 registered drug addicts in 1993.
- In the UK about 150 people died in one year using solvents. Some were first-time users.
- Man-made drugs were created for medical purposes only and have been around since 1903.

GAMBLING

'I started gambling on the machines when I was 12 years old because I was bored. Now it's got to the point where I do it all day every weekend because I think I'm going to win the jackpot. The most I've ever

won is £100 but I put that all back in because I thought
I was on a winning streak. Of course, I wasn't and I
lost it all.'
Lucy (14)

Around 66% of teenagers gamble to some degree,
whether it's through arcade games, electronic games or
on horses and/or dogs. While for many young people
gambling remains an occasional habit like going to
the cinema, 3% of these people develop a serious
addiction. Gambling is often called the hidden addiction because gamblers are very good about lying and
can explain away their need for money and their lack
of money very easily.

If you are worried that you may be becoming
addicted or have a friend that may be addicted, the
following signs all point to a possible problem:

- Gambling alone for long periods.
- A feeling that all your problems will be solved if
  you won 'X' amount of money.
- Being unable to stop gambling whether you win
  or lose.
- No limit on how much you gamble.
- Forming a 'relationship' with a particular venue,
  machine, or routine.
- Feeling remorse for putting your family through
  your addiction.
- Being unable to keep away from gambling.
- Mood swings, irritability and restlessness.
- Gambling becomes the only interest.

Emotional effects

Compulsive gambling is more than just having an urge to play games or to bet. It is about escape, just like any other addiction, and being forced to keep away can result in similar anxieties to that of an alcoholic – depression, frustration, etc. Gamblers end up losing their friends, their family and eventually even their jobs when their gambling ceases to be a social activity and becomes a way of life. Truanting from school is likely to happen, as is borrowing and not paying back money. Over time a deep depression may set in and a gambler may feel the only way out is suicide.

If you know someone who is addicted to gambling, try not to condemn them. Instead set them boundaries for what they can and cannot do in your relationship. For instance, make it clear that you won't lend them money but that you do care about them. Don't take responsibility for their gambling and its consequences. Above all encourage them to seek professional help.

Giving up

Don't wait to reach what is known as 'rock bottom' before you seek help. Don't wait until you're kicked out of school or your home or until you have to commit a crime before you get help. Addictions can occur at any age, and so can recovery.

Further information
Contact the UK Forum of Young People and Gambling (a national centre for information, advice and practical help for people addicted to gambling), Gamblers

Anonymous, or Gam-Anon (sister organization to Gamblers Anonymous, which provides help and support for friends, family and parents of gamblers). Contact details are in 'Resources'.

- Total gaming turnover in 1993 was £3.2 billion.
- £95 million is spent on slot machines alone.
- In the UK, half the homes with children have computer games.

Chapter Eight

ALTERNATIVE HEALTH

'What's all this stuff about oils, and sticking needles into your body? Does it really work, or is it a load of mumbo-jumbo?'
Selena (16)

What is alternative health? What can it do for you? You may have heard of the various therapies that are a part of alternative or complementary medicine, but do you really know what they can do for you?

It may sound like a load of rubbish to you but thousands of people worldwide swear by alternative medicine. Even people who work within traditional medicine are now seeing the benefits that this type of medicine can bring to general health care. However, before you rush off and opt for acupuncture instead of your GP, do bear in mind a couple of things. First, complementary medicine is very costly and works over a number of sessions; it won't be of much use to you if you only go once. Second, it is not available on the NHS unless you have a very serious illness. If you do decide to try it, always remember to make sure you let your GP know what you are doing beforehand. This way you know you won't be doing yourself any harm.

This is also important from the alternative practitioner's point of view because they will need a full medical history from you before they treat you. They will also ask you questions on your diet, family medical history, sleep patterns and emotional health. Just as it's important to always be honest with a doctor, it is important to be honest with a practitioner. They cannot treat you properly unless they know all the facts regarding your condition. All information is confidential.

With so much now being written about alternative health it's easy to think you can treat yourself. However, if you attempt to use a therapy you know little about, it can be dangerous and you can end up hurting yourself. Certain aromatherapy oils can poison you if misused, and it is always dangerous to use herbs if you know nothing about them. In order to make sure your health is in good hands, make sure your practitioner is qualified; check their qualifications before you let them treat you. The British Register of Complementary Practitioners (available from the Institute of Complementary Medicine – see 'Resources') provides a national listing of qualified practitioners in all the major therapies.

Acupuncture

Acupuncture is an ancient way of healing. It is Chinese in origin and has been around for over 2,500 years. It is based on the idea that specific areas of the skin are linked to the organs of the body. The energy of the body (the Chi) is distributed through twelve main energy lines (also known as meridians) and each of these pathways is linked to an organ. The blockage or under- or over-use of a particular pathway is thought to cause the relevant organ to work inefficiently and therefore cause illness.

The way an acupuncturist will discover which pathway needs assistance is by checking your pulses (each organ has a pulse – not just the heart) at your wrist, and by examining your facial colour, odour, tongue and emotional state.

Treatment is then carried out by stimulating the energy of the relevant pathway with the insertion of fine needles and warmth into the acupuncture point. The insertion of a needle is not painful, though you may feel a slight sensation at first, and another when it reaches the energy line. The needles are completely sterile and a high level of hygiene is adhered to at all times. The needle is kept in place for any time from two minutes to 45 minutes and then it is painlessly removed.

Though acupuncture has been shown to help specific conditions such as depression, anxiety, asthma and weight loss, its effect does more than simply heal your actual problem. Good acupuncture aims to restore your body's balance and make you feel emotionally and physically better.

All British acupuncturists should be members of one of five organizations that make up the Council for Acupuncture. Check for the relevant abbreviations – BAAR, CSAS, IROM, RTCM and TAS. For further information contact the Traditional Acupuncture Society or the Council for Acupuncture (see 'Resources').

• Acupuncture has been around for over 2,500 years: acupuncture needles were developed during 1766–1154 BC.
• There are three million Acupuncturists worldwide.

Aromatherapy

Aromatherapy is based on the use of essential oils taken from bark, leaves, seeds, flowers and roots of plants and herbs. These oils are then used to heal, as many have powerful antibiotic, anti-infectious and anti-spasmodic properties. They also affect the mind through the sense of smell: the link between smell and memory is crucial to helping functions such as sleep patterns and appetite in the body.

Aromatherapy is perhaps the best-known of all alternative therapies, but because it is so widely available in shops many people think they can just use the oils any way they like. However, there are a number of essential oils that can be harmful. Oils such as lemon, orange and citrus should never be used before going sunbathing or using a sunbed, as they will cause you to burn once they react with sunlight. Oils such as clove and cinnamon can also damage your skin. Every oil has to be mixed with sunflower oil, almond oil or a plain moisturizer before using as it is very dangerous to use a neat oil on your skin. And *never* take an oil internally.

That aside, and especially with the help of a trained therapist, aromatherapy can help conditions such as PMS, depression, insomnia, anxiety and skin conditions. For further information contact the International Federation of Aromatherapists (See 'Resources').

- Aromatherapy oils were first used in 10th century Arabia: the essential oils became known as the Perfumes of Arabia.
- Essential oils were brought to Europe by the Knights of the Crusade in the 12th century.

Homeopathy

Homeopathy is one of the few therapies available on the NHS. It works on the principle that 'like cures like', which means treating an illness with a substance that would give a healthy person similar symptoms to those displayed by the person who is ill. Homeopathy sees the symptoms of an illness as the body's reaction against the illness as it attempts to overcome it, and seeks to stimulate and not suppress this reaction.

It is a natural healing process in which the remedies (made up of herbs, minerals and even diseased tissues) are used in tiny proportions to assist the person to regain health by stimulating the body's natural healing forces. Homeopathic remedies are completely safe and non-addictive, with no side effects. It is practised by doctors who are fully qualified through conventional medicine and is recognized by the General Medical Council.

For further information contact the British Homeopathic Association (see 'Resources').

> • Homeopathy was known to the Greeks in the fifth
> century.
> • Homeopathic prescriptions are available under the
> NHS.

Osteopathy

Osteopathy involves the correcting of structural
defects in the spine to heal other parts of the body. The
idea is that the problems within the spine affect nerve
and blood flow to other areas of the body, causing
aches, pains and muscle spasms. The technique
involves manipulations and massage. Often a therapist
will locate the problem and then massage the area.
They will then set right the defect by a series of thrusts
and pulls. You may hear a loud click when the spine is
repositioned but the treatment is not painful.

Osteopathy is now widely recognized and accepted
by conventional medicine, and can help with everything from back pain to migraines, digestive disorders
to period pains. For further information contact the
British School of Osteopathy (see 'Resources').

> • Osteopathy was invented in 1874.

Chiropractice

Chiropractice is very similar to osteopathy as it involves manipulating the spine and other areas of the body. Unlike an osteopath, a chiropractor will use X-rays to aid diagnosis. Apart from that, the difference is simply in academic qualifications. For further information contact the British Chiropractic Association (see 'Resources').

Transcendental Meditation

Transcendental Meditation (also known as TM) is a technique of deep relaxation which enables you to deal with the stress and worry in your life. It is practised twice a day for 20 minutes, once in the morning and once in the evening, and can be done by anyone.

TM is widely used for improving health and energy, reducing stress and improving mental performance. Doctors now estimate that 80% of all people they see at a general practice surgery are suffering from a stress-related disorder, and TM has been proven to help these people deal with their problems. It has also been found to help with depression, anxiety, PMS and insomnia.

The wide-ranging benefits of TM on all areas of life have been validated by more than 450 scientific research studies in 24 different countries. The following have been listed as some of its benefits:

- Improvements in major factors associated with heart disease.
- Improvements in psychosomatic and stress disorders.
- Decreased anxiety and depression.

- Increased inner calm.
- Decreased irritability.

In order to learn how to practise TM you have to go to one of 80 centres around the UK and take a seven-step course. For further information contact Transcendental Meditation at the address in 'Resources'.

- Four million people practise Transcendental Meditation, including 160,000 in the UK.
- Transcendental Meditation has been found to be 1.5 to 8 times more powerful than any other programme in combating alcohol abuse, and 2 to 10 times more powerful in the case of cigarettes.
- In 1993 136 doctors wrote to the Health Minister asking for TM to be available on the NHS. Recently this has started to occur.

Naturopathy

The main principle of naturopathy is the importance of the body's natural health; this leads it towards self-cleansing and self-healing. The ideas behind this therapy are very different from those of traditional medicine. Naturopaths feel that illnesses are the body's efforts to get back to normal. Symptoms such as a cough, spots and fever are signs of a drive towards health and not an illness. For instance, a cough is seen to be cleaning out debris, a spot as clearing the skin. This is why a naturopath will not try to suppress symptoms.

Naturopathy is the original nutritional therapy and its basic premise is that healthy diet and living will prevent illness. Naturopaths feel that the body is very well equipped to withstand various kinds of changes and that this defence mechanism works on its own if nothing gets in its way. But when we feed our bodies with a bad diet, take no exercise, have bad posture and consume various drugs we do ourselves damage which cause us to become ill.

The way round this is to stop bad habits and do one or some of the following *under the care of a trained naturopath*:

- Change your diet – go on a natural, raw diet.
- Fasting – allow your body to deal with the illness and not focus on digestion.
- Adjustments to your posture – by massage or osteopathy.
- Hydrotherapy – this can include applications of hot and cold water.
- Exercise on a regular basis.

For further information contact the British College of Naturopathy (see 'Resources').

- Naturopathy traces its roots back to Hippocrates.

Herbalism

Herbs have been used all over the world for thousands of years to cure ailments and illnesses. Every culture, from the Indians of the Amazon Basin to Native

Americans and the Chinese, has well-developed forms of herbalism. Even in traditional medicine, many drugs have their basis in herbal medicine. It is important not to try and treat yourself; seek a trained herbalist who can take a detailed medical history and advise you on what to do. For further information contact the National Institute of Medical Herbalists (see 'Resources').

> • Aromatic oils have been used in Chinese herbalism for thousands of years – the 'Great Herbal' dates from around 200 BC and lists 365 plants used medicinally.

Reflexology

Reflexology is based on the idea that the body is divided into different zones, (five on each side of the body) which correspond to various parts of the underside of each foot. The actual technique involves the therapist massaging pressure points on the soles of the feet. This stimulates the nerve endings and triggers a reflex action in other organs throughout the body. This technique helps relax the patient and at the same time soothes sensitive areas throughout the body.

Therapists search for lumps and bumps under the skin and tenderness in the undersole. These lumps and various sore spots will highlight problem areas within your body. Reflexology helps many stress-related illnesses and it is extremely relaxing and soothing. It can also help with period problems and headaches.

For further information contact the Association of Reflexologists at the address in 'Resources'.

- Reflexology is 5,000 years old.
- Reflexology was introduced to Britain in the 1960s.

Chapter Nine

GENERAL HEALTH

Sometimes, no matter how healthy we are, we can be hit by an illness that's beyond our control. Perhaps it's something as ordinary as a cold or maybe it's an illness you've never heard of before. Perhaps what you've got isn't common and that makes you more scared to ask for help. Other times, you may have a strange itch or a painful lump and not know what to do about it. This is where your GP comes in. Even if you find out you have nothing whatsoever wrong with you, you should always seek help when you feel ill or worried. This way you can protect yourself and not be like the hundreds of people each year who leave it too late to get the help they need.

Of course, there are many illnesses that are so rare that they aren't very likely to attack someone of your health and age. However, this doesn't mean that you won't be touched by them in different ways. Perhaps a close friend, sibling, parent or other relative will get ill and you won't know how to cope. Maybe you're afraid that when you're older you'll get the illness too, or that you won't know what to do when an ill person needs your help.

In this chapter I will highlight some of the more common illnesses that may touch your life (however briefly) and show you where to go for help if something is affecting you or someone you know.

Asthma

'My sister has Asthma and we've been told to be careful around her. What is it and what happens when she has an attack?'
Julia (14)

Asthma is a distressing condition where tightness in the chest makes breathing difficult and painful. It affects nearly three million people in the UK. Asthma attacks can last for a few moments or over an hour, and a severe attack can last for several days, causing breathlessness, coughing and wheezing. During an attack, the muscles of the lungs go into an intense spasm and the bronchial tubes become inflamed and narrowed, making it difficult for the sufferer to inhale and exhale and causing shortness of breath. The air passages can then close to a minute size, making the sufferer feel like they are being suffocated. Recovery can then take anything from a couple of hours to a couple of days.

The attacks may be brought on by allergies to dust particles, pollen grains, mould spores and animals. Many modern factors are also responsible. Smoking and pollution are now known to bring on a range of allergic disorders. An attack can also be brought on by stress. Anyone with asthma, or who suspects they may have asthma, should see their GP so that the right drugs and prevention tactics can be prescribed.

Some modern drugs can alleviate asthma, especially ones which are taken through an inhaler; some people find using an inhaler every day can alleviate their asthma, but this does not work for everyone. For further information on what you can do to help your-self or the people you know who have asthma, contact the National Asthma Campaign (see 'Resources').

• 2,000 people die from asthma each year because they do not seek professional help.
• Yawning is a reflex action that occurs when the oxygen supply in your body's tissues is depleted.

Allergies

'I have strange rashes all over my arms and legs. I have never had them before and I don't feel ill but they do itch and look ugly. What can they be?'
Ellie (16)

'I have started using allergy-tested make-up because my skin is so sensitive but I am still getting itchy rashes. Why?'
Louise (16)

An allergy is an abnormal reaction to often harmless substances (allergens) which are inhaled, swallowed, injected or which touch the skin. You can be allergic to just about anything and it doesn't have to show itself in the way that you think. It's also quite possible to suddenly become allergic to something you have used for years, or to find yourself allergic to allergy-tested products.

Allergies can appear as rashes, sneezing, sore throats, sore eyes, nausea, diarrhoea, hives, itching, runny noses, etc. An allergy is your body's way of reacting against a substance it deems foreign. When this happens it sends antibodies to protect you, and the symptoms you end up with are a direct result of the antibodies reacting with the substance.

You may know you have an allergy to *something* and yet not know exactly what's causing it. If this occurs the only way you can find it is through a process of elimination. For instance, if you have a skin rash, try changing things like your soap powder, deodorant, soaps, creams, perfume, etc. If you keep sneezing, try changing where you go, keep out of smoky atmospheres, get your boyfriend or friends to stop wearing a particular brand of aftershave or perfume, etc. But remember to do these things one at a time or else your symptoms will disappear and you still won't be able to tell what was causing your initial problem.

There are also allergy clinics, where a specialist can find your specific allergy by giving you skin tests, but again this process takes time. Your GP or pharmacist may be able to help treat your allergy with antihistamines; these will relieve itchiness and soreness but won't get to the root of your problem. Try to help yourself by keeping away from things that give you bad reactions no matter how much you crave them.

Hay fever

'I have hay fever and every year it drives me crazy. What can I do?'
Toni (16)

Hay fever is an allergy to dust or pollen, which is why most people suffer in the summer when the grass pollen count is high. It affects nearly 10% of the population and is caused by the over-production of mucus after inhaling grass, pollen, dust or pollutants. It is also known as seasonal allergic rhino-conjunctivitis because it affects the nose and eyes at particular times of the year. Symptoms include irritation, itching, swelling and a blocked nose. The main ways to treat hay fever are:

- Staying away from pollen. Grass pollen levels are highest on hot sunny days, so it's best to stay inside mid-morning and late afternoon.
- Medicines such as antihistamines are widely used to stop allergic reactions. A few side effects may include headaches, dry mouth, skin rashes and upset stomachs.

In order to find the right relief see your GP. For further information and advice on hay fever contact the National Asthma Campaign (see 'Resources').

- Colds are caused by one of over 200 different viruses.
- There is no cure for the common cold.
- A sneeze can travel at 100 mph.

Hives

Hives can look like an allergic reaction. They are usually itchy and lumpy and often resemble a nettle rash. They are a sign of extreme stress and nervousness and will appear when you are worried. They can be treated with antihistamines to relieve the itching and welts, but prevention is again the best cure. Try to pinpoint when your hives appear. Is it near your exams? Or when you feel anxious in a crowd? Finding the answer to when they appear will help you worry less and avoid them.

Eczema

'I have really dry itchy skin and have been told it is eczema. Could you tell me more?'
Lorna (16)

Eczema is one of the main causes of dry and sensitive skin. It often appears as an inflamed rash that itches like crazy. There are many different types of eczema but they all have the same symptoms. Atopic eczema is more commonly found in babies and children. Seborrhoeic eczema is fairly common in younger adults; it tends to affect the scalp, face, groin and chest.

Eczema cannot be caught from other people but because the skin of an eczema sufferer is often cracked and broken it needs special attention and care to protect it from possible infection. See your GP for an exact diagnosis. Once diagnosed, eczema can be treated by emollients (simple moisturizers) and steroids, and through prevention. This means wearing comfortable cotton clothing and avoiding over-heating of the skin.

For further information contact the National Eczema Society (see 'Resources').

> • One person in ten has eczema at some point in their life.

Shingles

'My friend recently got shingles and it looked horrific. She said it was linked to chicken pox. I've had chicken pox so does this mean I could get it too?'
Rebecca (15)

The shingles virus is also known as herpes zoster virus. It infects the nerve endings in certain areas of the skin and causes a very painful blister-like rash. It is the same virus that causes chicken pox, so it does tend to affect people who have had chicken pox as the virus can lie dormant and later return when an individual is stressed. But this isn't always the case and just because you've had chicken pox doesn't mean you're going to get shingles. Shingles is also very common among people who have weak immune systems. If you think you may have shingles it is very important to seek professional medical help to alleviate the symptoms.

> • Shingles affects 3 in 100 people.

Glandular fever

'I have glandular fever and have been told not to overdo things. But the simplest things I do make me feel really tired and depressed.'
Sue (15)

Glandular fever used to be known as the kissing disease because it was thought that this was how the virus was passed from person to person. You don't need to kiss a person to get glandular fever, and not everyone who comes into contact with someone who has the virus will get it. It is now thought that people who are run down and exhausted are more likely to contract the illness.

If you have glandular fever you are likely to feel exhausted and tired all the time. You may sleep a great deal, lose your appetite and feel drained. Your glands may swell, you may get headaches and neck-aches and feel like you are walking around in a fog. You may also find that you have a sore throat and feel depressed.

However, if you want to find out for sure you must go along to your GP and have a blood test. Once diagnosed, the best way to recover is to have plenty of rest and a vitamin-enriched diet to help build up your immune system. If you look after yourself and do what your doctor says you can recover within a couple of weeks, though some people find it takes much longer for them to get back to a normal healthy life.

Bed-wetting: nocturnal enuresis

'I am 15 years old and I still wet the bed. It is so embarrassing. It means I can never stay over at friends' houses and I can't go on school holidays. I can't tell anyone but my parents. I worry that I'll always be like this and won't ever be able to have a proper relationship with anyone.'
Lesley (15)

This is more common a problem than you may think. Bed-wetting (or nocturnal enuresis) affects over half a million children. Many factors have been associated with bed-wetting, from stress to too much urine being produced at night. It is not a disease but its effects include:

- Teasing and rejection.
- Depression.
- Tension, worry and anxiety.
- Low self-esteem.
- Withdrawal.

Enuresis is no laughing matter and if not treated, its effects can be quite devastating. Research has shown that enuresis is related to one stage of sleep – the deep sleep stage. It is thought that this stage may be so deep that muscle control is lost and urination occurs.

There are many ways to deal with enuresis. Some clinics specialize in using alarms that wake the sleeper during the night while bed-wetting is occurring. This process enables the patient to learn how to control their bladder at night.

Some doctors may prescribe drugs which reduce the

amount of urine you produce overnight. In order to find out what works best for you and what you and your family can do, contact ERIC, the Enuresis Resource and Information Centre (see 'Resources').

• One million people suffer from bed-wetting.

Stammering

'My boyfriend has a stammer and I want to know how to help him to overcome it.'
Lena (16)

Stammering (or stuttering) is an involuntary repetition which blocks the normal flow of speech. It affects over 500,000 people in the UK alone. There is no single cause for stammering; some researchers believe that stammerers have difficulty in co-ordinating their muscles for speech, others believe it could be hereditary, while some feel it's an emotional response to outside pressure. It is probably a combination of physical and emotional factors coming together at the same time. There is no miracle cure for stammering but there are a number of things you can do to help yourself. Speech therapy will help you to develop confidence, social skills, and self-awareness. It will show you how not to panic in situations, and show you how to breathe and look at people when you speak.

For further information, contact the Association for Stammerers (AFS) or the Michael Palin Centre for Stammering Children (see 'Resources').

• Winston Churchill, Marilyn Monroe and King George VI were all stammerers.

Food poisoning

'I ate something at a barbecue the other day and was really sick for three days. My mum says it was food poisoning. How did I get it?'
Jill (15)

Food poisoning is the general term to describe illnesses caused by eating food infected by bacteria, e.g. salmonella. Infected food doesn't have to smell 'off' in order to give you food poisoning. Uncooked frozen food, badly re-heated food or food that has passed its 'use-by' date can all make you ill. The symptoms of food poisoning are mainly vomiting and/or diarrhoea, but according to what you have eaten you may also suffer from fever and stomach cramps.

The duration of the illness also depends on what you have eaten and how much of it you ate. Some cases last for a couple of hours, others for a few weeks. It's important with food poisoning to make sure you don't dehydrate; therefore drink plenty of plain water while you are ill. Though most food poisoning cases resolve themselves, some do need medical attention. This is why it's important to see your GP and find out whether you need antibiotics.

The best cure, of course, is prevention. This means maintaining high standards of hygiene around food:

- Make sure that all cold food is kept refrigerated.
- Always wash your hands after you've been to the lavatory.
- Don't re-freeze thawed frozen food.
- Wash salads and fruit thoroughly before eating.
- Cook meat thoroughly.
- Check use-by dates.
- Cook red kidney beans before eating in order to remove toxins.
- Don't eat uncooked eggs.
- Be very careful when re-heating foods.

Worms

'I have noticed small white things when I go to the toilet. I think they are worms and I am terrified of them. They are so itchy, what can I do?
Jenny (15)

Worms (also known as Enterobius vermicularis) are a very common condition. The actual worms are tiny and inhabit the gut of about one in three of us, most of the time. They mainly live in the area near your appendix and they come out at night and lay their eggs on the skin around your bottom, which is why they are itchy.

They can be caught from eating uncooked food and from other human beings, which is why it's important to be scrupulously clean all the time. Always wash your hands thoroughly, especially under the nails after you've been to the toilet, and before you handle food. This way you won't re-infect yourself. Remember you can pass worms on to your family, so seek help. Your doctor or pharmacist can give you anti-worm medication that will clear up the worms and get rid of the discomfort.

Irritable bowel syndrome

'I get a really bad pain in my stomach and then my stomach bloats out. I also get diarrhoea and constipation. Is this IBS?'
Erica (17)

Irritable bowel syndrome (IBS) is a very common digestive disorder that brings misery to many people. Its main symptoms are abdominal pain, diarrhoea or constipation, bloating and wind. The pain can be felt throughout the abdomen and it is often worst in the morning. Estimates vary as to how many people have IBS but it could well affect 40% of the population.

The causes of IBS are still largely unknown. It has been suggested that IBS is caused by a disorder of the bowel muscle and/or that people who suffer from IBS may have an over-sensitive bowel which can be triggered by stress and worry. There is nothing that cures all the symptoms of IBS but there are various treatments which can ease some of them. Diet, relaxation techniques and help from your GP can all work together to help alleviate some of your pain. For further information contact the British Digestive Foundation at the address in 'Resources'.

> • Indigestion is usually caused by eating food that is too rich or fatty, or by eating too fast and too much. Symptoms include wind, bloating and cramps.

Cancer

'I know cancer in teenagers isn't common, but you hear about cancer all the time and it's really scary. How can I stop myself from getting it in later life?'
Tina (16)

Cancer is a disease of individual cells that can attack any organ or tissue in your body. It occurs when something goes wrong inside a cell which stops the cell from growing properly. There is now some evidence that low-fat, high-fibre diets can be helpful in reducing the risks for *some* types of cancer. But it is undoubtedly smoking which causes the most deaths from cancer. Nine out of ten cases of lung cancer are due to smoking, and lung cancer alone causes one third of all cancer deaths in Britain. So your best bet is to keep away from cigarettes.

Despite the fact that cancer can be fatal, if the cancer is detected early, the chances of ridding your body of it are high. For instance, skin cancer (melanoma) is 95% curable in the early stages. Ovarian/cervical cancer is also curable if caught in the early stages.

In order to protect yourself, check your body for lumps. If you discover any lump in your body that worries you or has just appeared or hurts, then for your own peace of mind get it checked out. Remember, once you start having sex it is important to get regular cervical smears (every three years). This is because long before cervical cancer is established there are detectable changes in the cells around the neck of the womb (cervix). A cervical smear is a simple and easy test that is performed in order to detect abnormalities in these cells. For further information contact the Women's National Cancer Control Campaign (see 'Resources').

> • There are over 200 different types of cancer.

Diabetes

'My friend has just been told she has diabetes. I don't know anything about it and I don't know how to help her.'
Sue (15)

Diabetes occurs when the amount of glucose in the blood is too high and the body can't use it properly. Insulin, a hormone produced by the pancreas, is needed to convert this glucose into the energy that the body needs. If the pancreas does not produce enough insulin, or if the body can't use the insulin, then diabetes occurs. There are two types of diabetes:

- Insulin dependent diabetes; occurs before the age of 40 and is treated by insulin injections.
- Non-insulin dependent diabetes; usually diagnosed after 40 and treated by diet and tablets.

The symptoms of diabetes include excessive thirst, weight loss, frequent urination, and constant tiredness. If you have such symptoms you need to go for a blood and urine test at your doctor's.

Diabetes, if not treated properly, can lead to problems with the heart, kidneys and eyes. It is not contagious, nor is it the result of eating too many sweet things. Diabetics lead perfectly normal and healthy lives. However, blood sugar levels have to be controlled. This is done with insulin injections, but because it is hard to calculate how much insulin is needed, frequent monitoring of the blood is also necessary.

Other things you will have to do are exercise, watch your diet, eat on schedule and not skip any meals. This means no junk food, sugar or alcohol. It is important to be controlled about what you eat and not try to rebel against this illness because it *is* life threatening. Life as a diabetic is tough but you can live a healthy and fun life like everyone else with just a little extra care.

For more help and further information contact the British Diabetic Association (see 'Resources').

• Over one million people in the UK have diabetes. 60,000 new cases are diagnosed each year.

Epilepsy

'I am an epileptic and it really worries me. I know a bit about epilepsy but I worry that no one else under-

stands. I had a seizure once and everyone treated me as if I were mentally ill.'
Fiona (15)

Epilepsy is a term used to describe a disorder of the central nervous system. The disorder causes seizures but it is *not* a mental illness and it is *not* contagious. No one quite knows why some people have epilepsy and others don't, but research is going on all the time. Until a cure is found, seizures can be controlled by medication and you can lead a perfectly healthy life.

If you are in the presence of someone having an epileptic seizure don't force a hard object between their teeth (this is a myth) or give them anything to eat or drink. Just loosen their clothing and make sure they are safe from harm. Most seizures last a few minutes and then the sufferer will come round. For further information contact the British Epilepsy Association (see 'Resources').

> • Epilepsy affects one in 200 people.

Multiple Sclerosis (MS)

'My mum has just been diagnosed with MS. What is it and is it infectious?'
Mira (15)

MS is the most common disease involving the central nervous system (i.e. the brain and the spinal cord). Anyone can develop the condition, but it is not infectious and not hereditary. At present doctors do not know why some people get MS and others don't.

MS occurs due to a breakdown of the coating (myelin) around the nerves in the body. This interferes with messages from the brain to other parts of the body, causing varying symptoms in the sufferer. Lack of co-ordination, blindness, fatigue, numbness and memory problems can all occur. However, the severity of the symptoms vary from person to person. For most of the time the disease is one of relapses and remissions. Attacks are followed by periods of partial or full recovery. A minority of people become severely disabled but the majority of people with MS lead normal lives. MS itself is not fatal and the majority of sufferers have a normal life expectancy.

At present there is no treatment available for MS, but individual symptoms can be treated. For further information contact the MS Society (see 'Resources').

- 80,000 people in the UK are affected with MS.
- The usual age of onset for MS is between 20 and 35 years old.
- In rare cases it can affect people as young as 12 years old.

Chapter Ten

EMOTIONAL HEALTH

We all want to be healthy people but sometimes, due to circumstances beyond our control, our lives are thrown into disarray and we no longer know if what we're experiencing is natural or even normal. I know people who refuse to cry when they're upset because they think it's weak. People who refuse to get angry and show their temper because they think no one will like them. Others who shout all the time because they're frustrated and unhappy and can't explain what's really bothering them. But then I also know people who aren't afraid to say when they are upset and when they feel depressed, and people who openly display their grief to anyone and everyone. Who's right and who's wrong?

Is it healthy to be angry, to lose your temper, to cry when you're upset, to feel envious of your friends and to make mistakes? Of course it is!

And is it healthy and normal to feel that no one will understand and that what you're experiencing is so rare that you can't talk about it? Of course it is!

There is no right and wrong when it comes to emotions – you feel what you feel – but the key to coping is learning to be open about your experiences. To speak up when you're being trodden on. To ask for help when you're being hurt and to cry on people's shoulders when someone is mean to you.

Growing up is a confusing thing, and it's difficult to

know how to deal with the things that happen to us, especially if we've never come across them before. None of us have an inbuilt mechanism to cope when things go very wrong in our lives. How are we supposed to know how to cope with heartbreak and loss? Or bullying and abuse? The important thing is always to remember that while you may not feel able to deal with your problems, lots of other people can help you. People who have gone through the same thing you're going through, or trained professionals, or the people you know and love. No matter how low and miserable you feel, you are never alone.

FEELING HEARTBROKEN

'My boyfriend ditched me over a year ago and I still haven't got over him. I don't know what's wrong with me. I still cry over him every night. I can't face going out with someone else and I worry that I'll always feel this way.'
Fiona (17)

'Ever since I broke up with my boyfriend my life has changed. I am depressed all the time. I can't see any point to the future. I feel insecure, unconfident and ugly. People say I'll get over him and meet someone new but I don't know if I will.'
Justine (15)

Heartbreak is a natural emotional response to loss. It occurs due to the demise of a close intimate relationship (whether it was your choice or not) with someone you love. Its effects are very similar to those of bereavement because you are literally grieving a loss. People who are heartbroken speak of depression, lethargy, loss of appetite or gained appetite. They talk of how there's 'no point' to anything and of an overwhelming sadness.

Being chucked by someone you love is hard. If they blamed you, or went off with someone else, it's doubly hard to get over. However, it's important to realize that just because they left you, it doesn't mean that you're worthless or that you've changed. Sadly, messy endings do happen and there's nothing you can do about it. You can try to get your ex to explain things more fully to you, but not everyone can be open when a relationship ends, and more often than not you'll be left with conflicting emotions.

The only way to deal with heartbreak is to grieve. This involves giving yourself time to get over what has happened. Don't jump into a new relationship or pretend everything is OK when it isn't. Lots of people think it's indulgent to go around being heartbroken for longer than a week, but there's nothing wrong in feeling bad for a while. Allowing yourself adequate time and space to deal with things is the only way forward. By all means, think bad thoughts, cry, feel regret and feel angry. This won't last for ever and you'll eventually accept what has happened and move on. After all, this experience will eventually make you feel better and stronger about yourself. You can and will survive heartbreak and you can and will go on to love again.

If you can't get over your ex, it could be because you would rather stay unhappy thinking about him than not think about him at all. Lots of people do this when they are heartbroken because they know that when they let go of the pain their relationship really is over once and for all. If you feel this way you may need counselling to find a way out and get over what has happened.

FEELING DESPERATE – ABUSE

Abuse comes in lots of different forms. It can occur when adults hurt young people – either physically or in some other way. There are four main areas of abuse.

- Physical – including hitting, kicking, punching and burning.
- Emotional – including threats, swearing and degradation; all things which will undermine your confidence.
- Neglect – when basic needs such as food, warmth, shelter and medical care are not given.
- Sexual – when an adult pressurizes or forces a young person to take part in any kind of sexual activity.

All forms of abuse are damaging. No one quite knows why some adults abuse children. In some cases, the abuser may have been abused in the same way as a child. Other people do it because they are stressed or have problems, and some do it because they have addictions to drink or drugs. Whatever their reason, the abuse is always wrong and never *ever* the young person's fault.

Sexual abuse

'I am being sexually abused by my uncle and I'm too afraid to do anything. I think it may be my fault or that I encouraged him in some way. He keeps telling me how attractive I am and that's why he can't keep away.'
Anon (13)

Child sexual abuse occurs when an adult or older person touches or uses a child in a sexual way. It's always wrong because your body is yours and yours alone. No one (no matter who they are) has the right to touch it without your consent, abuse it or hurt you in any way.

Incest is when the abuser is part of the immediate family. Many victims say the results of it appear in physical and psychological forms. What's more, because it's such a taboo subject victims often feel they are alone, but figures now show that it is more widespread than anyone previously thought. If it is happening to you, you *must* seek help. People will believe you and no one will blame you: sexual abuse is never the victim's fault. If you feel you can't turn to someone you know well, contact ChildLine, your local social services (number in directory), a teacher, a friend's parent, Rape Crisis or the NSPCC Child Protection Helpline (see 'Resources').

Young abused people are only taken away from their families in a very small number of cases (unless they ask to be removed), when it is actually considered dangerous for them to stay at home. Most then return home, just as soon as it is felt they will be safe.

If you know that abuse is going on, whether it be to a friend, boyfriend, girlfriend or neighbour, ring any helpline and seek help for them. You must act, as violent abuse and assault can leave children with physical disabilities and can scar their emotional growth.

Further information
For help, advice and information, contact ChildLine, the NSPCC Helpline, NCH Action for Children, or Victim Support. (See 'Resources' for details.)

FEELING LOSS – BEREAVEMENT

'I lost my mum in a car accident last year and even now I can't believe she's gone. I wake up every day and expect to find her calling me or making breakfast. When I realize she's dead, I find myself crying and getting depressed. Some days I just stay in bed and refuse to go out. Other days I pretend she's not really gone but on holiday and will be back soon. My brother and father refuse to talk about it. They say I can't afford to dwell on things and I have to just forget it. But how can I? She's my mum, I can't just forget her.'
Tina (17)

No one likes talking about death. People feel it's creepy and scary and somehow morbid. But death is part of nature, and refusing to have anything to do with it makes life for bereaved people extremely hard. In the same way, worrying about when you're going to die and/or about losing the people you love achieves nothing. All it does is stop you from enjoying the present. If you're afraid of death, talking to people can help you to see it from a different perspective and one that isn't so scary. Remember also that people are living longer and longer: you and most of the people you know could very well live to be 110 years old.

If you've lost someone you are probably in a lot of pain. Maybe you feel lost, scared and alone. Maybe you feel that no one understands. Losing someone you love is perhaps the most painful and distressing loss you will ever have to go through, but you don't have to do it on your own. If there is no one you can turn to and your family won't discuss it, you can turn to an outside counsellor for help. (Contact CRUSE or your GP).

Grief itself is a complicated process. It has four main stages – shock, anger, depression and acceptance.

The shock may leave you feeling completely numb and empty. Life may appear unreal and somewhat foggy. You may even find it hard to cry and people may make you feel bad for this; if they do, ignore them. You will cry when you're ready and in any case, tears aren't the only way to express grief. In a way, shock has its value; it helps to protect you in the early days when you have to go through the practical arrangements of a death. Later you may find yourself searching for or dreaming about the person who has died. Perhaps you'll imagine seeing them walk down the street or you may hear them call your name. If this happens, try not to think that you're going mad; this reaction will fade over time as you begin to accept that the person has really gone.

You may then find yourself becoming really angry. Angry with the person who has died. Angry with yourself for not being there or saving them from death. You may also feel depressed, unwell, irritable, suffer from insomnia, lose your appetite or start having panic attacks. All these are natural responses and you can learn to deal with them by seeking counselling help.

Sometimes the way that you grieve someone will depend on how they died. Anger can appear much earlier if it was a senseless accident or a terminal illness. You may feel, 'How unfair', or 'Why them?' It is especially hard when someone kills themselves. However, it's important to realize that people who kill themselves do so out of desperation, frustration and an inability to see a way out of their present situation. They don't do it because they had a fight with a friend or were annoyed with their girl/boyfriend. Suicide is a desperate bid for escape from a world they can't deal with. Sadly, such a death can leave everyone distressed and guilt-ridden, no matter how vaguely they knew the dead person. This is because there is always a feeling that a suicide could have been prevented.

Coming to terms with such losses takes time, so be patient with yourself. In time you won't think about the person you lost so much and when you do, you won't always feel sad about them. Grieving takes time, and that time is nearly always longer than people expect. It comes in waves and some days can be very bad, but gradually the distress will lessen and you will be able to go and build your life without the person you lost, remembering them in a positive way.

Further information
CRUSE (Bereavement Care) offers confidential counselling to all bereaved young people. You could also contact the National Association of Bereavement Services. See 'Resources' for details.

FEELING SHY

'My shyness is ruining my life. I can't do anything because I feel like people will reject me or tell me I am useless. I haven't got any friends and no one speaks to me. It's got to the stage where I walk around with my head down all the time so I don't have to look at anyone.'
Tanya (14)

If you're so shy that you can't bring yourself to talk to anyone, you have to consider three things. One, no one is judging you or looking at you and waiting for you to fail. Two, if you don't make an effort with people they won't make an effort with you. Wandering around with your head down will make people think you're unfriendly, and even if they are friendly towards you, how will you know with your head down? Three, nearly everybody suffers from varying levels of shyness – other people's 'unfriendliness' is often a shy reaction to your own 'unfriendliness'.

No one is saying you have to suddenly become Miss Sociable, but in order to let people start seeing you, you have to be a bit assertive. Start trying to change by doing little things like smiling when you see someone you know. They might not smile back at first but after they get used to seeing you do it they'll start being friendlier. Say 'hello' whenever you can. If you're stuck for something to say in a conversation, ask people about themselves and listen to what others say, instead of panicking about what they may be thinking of you.

Often those of us who are shy are afraid to take a risk with people because we have too high an expectation of ourselves and of what other people expect. I knew a shy girl who didn't think people would like her because she wasn't funny! But no one expected her to be funny – they just wanted her to be herself. So what happens if you *do* do something embarrassing? Easy – first laugh, that will stop everyone, especially you, feeling uncomfortable. Then just start over. No one will think badly of you or call you a fool. It's more likely that they'll sympathize and be more friendly once they can see that you don't take yourself too seriously.

Remember: people like people who like themselves. No one wants to be friends with someone who always puts themself down. Where's the fun in that? We're all different after all: some of us are outgoing and witty, others quieter and more sensitive. Be yourself – that's all that matters.

FEELING ANGRY

'Everyone says that I have such a bad temper and I know they are right. I can't help it but things annoy me all the time. I'm always angry. What's wrong with me?'
Helen (15)

What makes you angry? Someone barging past you on the bus? A friend gossiping about you? A TV programme? A boyfriend who won't say 'I love you'? Noisy neighbours?

If any of the above stir something in you then you'll probably recognize the following physical reaction too. When you're angry your body will start to feel hot and flushed, you will sweat and your throat, chest and jaw will become tense. Your heart will pound and your breathing will become shallow. Basically this is all because your body is gearing up to take action. Not many people do then take action; they try to swallow their anger and repress it, which means it only comes back worse the next time.

Being angry with someone you love (like your parents, a sibling, a best friend, etc.) is fairly common. Anger is a normal healthy emotion, like joy or envy. Your teenage years are a time when you find that the things that you believe don't always coincide with what others may think. Believing that no one understands you (or is even willing to try) can lead to feelings of anger that can cause arguments. If you feel that your life is full of anger and you can't cope, then don't bottle up your fears. Scientific studies show that constantly repressed anger directly affects the immune system, leaving you open to all kinds of health problems. So try and make anger *work* for you instead:

- Learn to communicate, by looking at the situation and deciding what's really making you angry. For instance, is it the fact that someone doesn't agree with you that makes you mad or the fact that they don't take you seriously?
- Speak up for yourself and tell people when they upset you. Remember, bottled-up anger leads to headaches and stress-related illnesses.
- Don't waste your energy. There's no use getting mad just because the bus is late or you've lost something. If you lose your cool over simple

things no one will take you seriously when something is really up.

- Don't stew over what you should have said and done. Once you've had it out forget about it.
- Make sure your anger is justified.
- Vent your anger on other things. Scream into a pillow, kick a cardboard box, do some physical exercise.
- If you're very worried about controlling your temper, talk to your parents or to someone you trust, and explain how you feel. And if you come from a family which fights all the time you could always seek family counselling. Parent Network (see 'Resources') provide Parent-Link support groups for parents and children who need help.

FEELING ALONE – RUNNING AWAY

'I can't bear living at home any longer. My mum and I fight constantly and it's awful. I know I'd be better off living somewhere else but she won't let me go. My only option is to run away.'
Gaby (15)

The National Children's Home estimate that 43,000 young people aged 17 and under ran away in 1990 alone. Most of these young people cited family problems as their reason for running away. The sad truth was that the majority of their problems weren't solved by leaving home. No matter how bad life is with your family, setting up your own home for the first time is a daunting task without money and a job. Being homeless is very rough. You are open to all kinds of risks and dangers.

Under the current law young people under 18 years old are not entitled to any state benefit and therefore if you can't pay your rent no one else will pay it for you, and if you don't have an address, how are you going to get a job?

Of course, this doesn't mean you have to stay at home no matter what. If you are being abused (see page 204) or your parents have chucked you out, then you must contact the Social Services (number in your local phone book) and they have to house you.

If you want to leave home because you hate it there, ask yourself what the real problem is and try to sort that out. If you can't deal with it on your own, then think about talking it through with a relative, an older person you trust or a professional counsellor (see below). Sometimes an outsider can help by bringing an objective viewpoint to your problems.

No matter how old or young you are, when you live with someone, a certain amount of friction is normal and natural. The key to getting by at home is communication. If you're angry that you have a sister who wrecks your things, don't take it out on your mum, say what's on your mind. Sometimes family fights can be about nothing at all. Perhaps you just don't get on with your parents any more. Maybe you don't agree on anything; that's OK. No one's saying you and your family have to agree on everything. Bear in mind that sometimes the people you live with will pick on you for no reason: one of the worst parts of living with people is that you take out your bad moods on each other.

It's all part of life, and if you run away every time things go wrong you'll never be able to sort out what's really worrying and upsetting you.

If you hate your life at home, take action and do something about it. Work towards solving your problems and your worries, if not with your parents then with someone you can trust and confide in.

Further information
For more help and advice, contact ChildLine, Parent Network, or Careline, a confidential counselling service for young people (see 'Resources').

HOW TO STAY EMOTIONALLY HEALTHY

Put an end to guilt

Some people feel to blame for the slightest thing that goes wrong whether or not it's their fault. They feel guilty when they let people down and guilty when someone does something bad to them. One way to stop feeling guilty is to stop taking responsibility for everyone else's happiness. If you go out with a person and they have a bad time then that's their problem not yours. If you're late and it's unavoidable then don't let it blow up to be a huge event; just apologize and move on. Another way to combat guilt is to not ponder on things that are in the past. For instance, don't keep feeling bad for being mean to someone: be nice to them from now on.

Learn to compromise

Some people think that a compromise is the same as giving in. They believe if you can't make things happen your way then you've lost. Accepting that you may not get everything you want means less stress and upset in the end. If you find yourself having the same bad feelings about a person over and over it may be time to assess where you are going wrong. You don't have to control everything to be happy. You can let other people take the lead now and again and compromise on a situation. If you hold out for every little thing, you could well end up feeling pretty lonely. It's also important to realize that sometimes there are arguments that you won't win; when this happens it helps if you can learn to lose gracefully.

Be assertive

There's a big difference between being assertive and being aggressive, and yet people often mix them up. To be assertive you don't have to raise your voice, or be pushy and you don't have to yell to get your way. In fact, there's nothing more likely to get a firm 'NO' than shouting in someone's face. If you want to get someone to see your point, construct a reasonable argument with valid points. Learning to stand up for yourself is an important part of becoming an adult. This means learning to say 'no' to the things you don't want to do, and not letting people manipulate you, bully you or put you down. If you're not sure how to go about this, try seeking help from people you admire and like. Watch how they handle situations and how they cope with the things you find tricky.

Don't expect perfection

Is your life a dream come true? If it is, then congratulations; if it isn't, then you're like the 99.99% of other people in this world. Life isn't perfect and no one escapes having to go through the ups and downs of it. If you keep trying to live up to unrealistically high expectations of always being happy, content and in love, then you are going to be disappointed. Accepting that life comes with bumps and bruises is a gigantic step forwards to becoming a healthy person.

Talk about how you feel

This doesn't mean you have to analyse everything you do, say and think. But it does mean you have to learn to talk when you're fed up and depressed; and to speak up when you feel you're being stepped on, not necessarily to the person who is doing it but definitely to someone. The key to coping with life is finding the balance between what you can deal with and what you can't. If there's no friend or family member you can confide in and talk to, you can contact any of the youth helplines. It isn't a failure to ask for help or see a counsellor, it's a positive and constructive thing to do. Often an outsider with objective eyes, who doesn't know you or your family, can be of more help than a friend or relative.

One confidential line is ChildLine: they won't tell your parents you called, and because they are a free phone number, the call won't appear on your parents' phone bill (unless it's a mobile phone). For face-to-face counselling contact Youth Access (see 'Resources'), who will give you details of your nearest youth counselling centre.

You are in control of your life

Above all remember that you are in control of your life. You can be anything you want to be. You are not helpless or at the mercy of others. Your parents may have some legal control of you now, but if they abuse that power you can do something about it. If you have teachers who always put you down you can report them and move classes. If you have a doctor who doesn't listen to you, you can see another doctor. All you need to do to be a healthy, happy and emotionally secure person is to do the best that you can for yourself, and to know that when you are out of your depth there are people you can turn to for help and advice.

Resources

INFORMATION AND HELPLINES

Acne Support Group
PO Box 230, Hayes, Middlesex UB4 9HW
Tel: 0891 318220

Adfam National
82 Old Brompton Road, London SW7 3LQ
Tel: 0171 823 9313
A national helpline supplying help and advice for the family
and friends of drug users.

Al-Anon Family Groups
61 Great Dover Street, London SE1 4YF

Alateen
61 Great Dover Street, London SE1 4YF
Tel: 0171 403 0888

Alcoholics Anonymous
Head Office, PO Box 1, Stonebow House, Stonebow,
York YO1 2NJ
Tel: 01904 644026

Alcohol Concern
Waterbridge House, 32–36 Loman Street, London SE1 0EE
Tel: 0171 928 7377

ASH (Action on Smoking and Health)
109 Gloucester Place, London W1H 3PH
Tel: 0171 935 3519

The Association of Reflexologists
110 John Silkin Lane, London SE8 5BE

Association for Stammerers (AFS)
St Margaret's House, 21 Old Ford Road, London E2 9PL
Tel: 0181 983 1003

Bristol Crisis Service for Women
PO Box 654, Bristol BS99 1XH
National Helpline: 0117 925 1119

British Agencies for Adoption and Fostering (BAAF)
11 Southwark Street, London SE1 1RQ
Tel: 0171 407 8800

British Association of Aesthetic Plastic Surgeons
The Royal College of Surgeons, 35–43 Lincoln's Inn Fields, London WC2A 3PN

British Association of Dermatologists
19 Fitzroy Square, London W1P 5HQ
Tel: 0171 383 0266

British Chiropractic Association
Premier House, 10 Greycoat Place, London SW1
Tel: 0171 222 8866

British College of Naturopathy
Frazer House, 6 Netherhall Gardens, London NW3 5RR
Tel: 0171 435 8728

British Dental Health Foundation
Eastlands Court, St Peter's Road, Rugby,
Warwickshire CV21 3QP
(Enclose an s.a.e.)

British Diabetic Association
10 Queen Anne Street, London W1M OBD
Tel: 0171 323 1531

British Digestive Foundation
3 St Andrew's Place, London NW1 4LB

British Epilepsy Association
Anstey House, 40 Hanover Square, Leeds LS3 1BE
Tel: 0345 089599

British Homeopathic Association
27a Devonshire Street, London W1N IRJ
Tel: 0171 935 2163

British Migraine Association
178a High Road, Byfleet, West Byfleet, Surrey KT14 7ED
Tel: 01932 352468

British Nutrition Foundation
High Holborn House, 52–54 High Holborn,
London WC1V 6RQ

British School of Osteopathy
1–4 Suffolk Street, London SW1Y 4HG
Tel: 0171 930 9254

British Pregnancy Advisory Service (BPAS)
Austy Manor, Wootton Wawen, Solihull,
West Midlands B95 6BX
Tel: 01564 793225

Brook Advisory Centres
Tel: 0171 713 9000
Phone for details of your nearest clinic.

Careline
Tel: 0181 514 1177
Confidential counselling service for young people.

ChildLine
Tel: 0800 1111

Council for Acupuncture
Suite 1, 19 Cavendish Square, London W1M 9AD
Tel: 0171 409 1440

CRUSE: Bereavement Care
126 Sheen Road, Richmond, Surrey TW9 1UR
Tel: 0181 940 4818 (for appointments)
Helpline: 0181 332 7227
Offers confidential counselling to all bereaved people.

Defeat Depression Campaign
17 Belgrave Square, London SW1X 8PG

Depression Alliance
PO Box 1022, London SE1 7QB
Tel: 0171 721 7672

Diet Breakers
Barford St Michael, Banbury, Oxon OX15 OUA
Tel: 01869 337070

Drinkline
Tel: 0345 320202

Eating Disorders Association
Sackville Place, 44 Magdalen Street, Norwich,
Norfolk NR3 1JE
Tel: 01603 621414

Resources

ERIC (Enuresis Resource and Information Centre)
65 St Michael's Hill, Bristol BS2 8DZ
Tel: 0117 926 4920

Family Planning Association
27–35 Mortimer Street, London W1N 7RJ
Tel: 0171 636 7866
Phone (9–5) for details of your nearest clinic.

Fellowship of Depressives Anonymous
36 Chestnut Avenue, Beverley, North Humberside HU17 9QU

First Steps to Freedom
22 Randall Road, Kenilworth, Warwicks CV8 1JY
Tel: 01926 851608

Foodsense
London SE99 7TT
Tel: 0645 556000

Gamblers Anonymous
17/23 Blantyre Street, Cheyne Walk, London SW10
Tel: 0171 352 3060

Gam-Anon
PO Box 88, London SW10 0EU
Tel: 0181 741 4181
Sister organization to Gamblers Anonymous. Provides help
and support for friends, family and parents of gamblers.

Herpes Association
41 North Road, London N7 9DP
Tel: 0171 609 9061

Institute of Complementary Medicine
PO Box 194, London SE16 1QZ
Tel: 0171 237 5165

International Federation of Aromatherapists
Department of Continuing Education, Royal Masonic
Hospital, Ravenscourt Park, London W6 0TN

Marie Stopes Association
Marie Stopes House, 108 Whitfield Street, London W1P 6BE
Tel: 0171 388 2585

Marie Stopes Health Clinics
Tel: 0171 388 4843
Phone for details of your nearest clinic.

Maisner Centre
PO Box 464, Hove, East Sussex BN3 2BN
Tel: 01273 729818

Michael Palin Centre for Stammering Children
Finsbury Health Centre, Pine Street, London EC1R OJH
Tel: 0171 837 0031

MIND (National Association for Mental Health)
Granta House, 15/19 Broadway, Stratford, London E15 4BQ
Tel: 0181 522 1728

MS Society
25 Effie Road, London SW6 1EE
Helpline: 0171 371 8000

Narcotics Anonymous
PO Box 1980, London N19 3LS
Tel: 0171 351 6794
Self-help group for drug users.

National AIDS Helpline
Tel: 0800 567123 (24 hours)

The National Association of Bereavement Services
20 Norton Folgate, London E1 6DB
Tel: 0171 247 1080

Resources

National Asthma Campaign
Providence Place, London N1 ONT
Helpline: 0345 010203

National Drugs Helpline
Tel: 0800 776600 (24 hours)
This confidential and sympathetic helpline is run by trained counsellors, and is available to anyone who has a question on drugs or drug-related issues. (Calls are totally free and won't appear on your phone bill.)

National Eczema Society
163 Eversholt Street, London NW1 1BU
Tel: 0171 399 4097

National Foster Care Association (NFCA)
Leonard House, 5–7 Marshalsea Road, London SE1 1EP
Tel: 0171 828 6266

National Institute of Medical Herbalists
41 Hatherley Road, Winchester, Hants SO22 6RR
Tel: 01962 68776

NSPCC Helpline
Tel: 0800 800500

NCH Action for Children
85 Highbury Park, London N5 1UD
Tel: 0171 226 2033

Parent Network
44–46 Caversham Road, London NW5 2DS
Tel: 0171 485 8535
Provides Parent-Link support groups for parents and children who need help.

PAX
4 Manorbrook, London SE3 9AW
Tel: 0181 318 5026

Phobics Society
4 Cheltenham Road, Chorlton-cum-Hardy,
Manchester M21 1QN
Tel: 0161 881 1937

Pregnancy Advisory Service
11–13 Charlotte Street, London W1P 1HD
Tel: 0171 637 8962

PREMSOC (The Pre-Menstrual Society)
PO Box 429, Addlestone, Surrey KT15 1DZ

QUIT (National Society of Non-Smokers)
102 Gloucester Place, London W1H 3DA
Helpline: 0171 487 3000

Relaxation for Living Trust
168–170 Oatlands Drive, Weybridge, Surrey KT13 9ET

Release
388 Old Street, London EC1V 9LT
Tel: 0171 603 8654
For details of local drug services in your area.

SAD Association
PO Box 989, London SW7 2PZ
Tel: 01903 814942

SANE
Tel: 0171 724 8000
Emergency helpline for relatives and sufferers from mental illness.

Resources

The Samaritans
Tel: 0345 909090 (local rates)

SCODA (Standing Conference on Drug Abuse)
1–4 Hatton Place, Hatton Garden, London EC1N 8ND
Tel: 0171 430 2341

Sports Council
Tel: 0171 388 1277

Tampax
Customer Services Dept, Tambrands Ltd, Dunsbury Way, Havant, Hants PO9 5DG
Write for information on tampons and periods.

Terrence Higgins Trust
Tel: 0171 242 1010

Toxic Shock Syndrome Information Service
24–28 Bloomsbury Way, London WC1A 2PX

Traditional Acupuncture Society
1 The Ridgeway, Stratford-upon-Avon, Warwickshire CV37 9JL

Transcendental Meditation
Freepost, London SW1 4YY
Tel: 0800 269 303

UK Forum of Young People and Gambling
11 St Bride Street, London EC4A 4AS
Tel: 0171 353 2366
National centre for information, advice and practical help for people addicted to gambling.

Victim Support
National Office, Cranmer House, 39 Brixton Road,
London SW9 6DZ
Tel: 0171 735 9166

Women's Nutritional Advisory Service
PO Box 268, Hove, East Sussex, BN3 1RW

Women's Nationwide Cancer Control Campaign (WNCCC)
Suna House, 128–130 Curtain Road, London EC2A 3AR
Send s.a.e. for a free leaflet on how to check out your breasts.

Youth Access
Ashby House, 62a Ashby Road, Loughborough,
Leicestershire LE11 3AE
Tel: 01509 210420 (9–5.30 weekdays)
Phone for details of local youth counselling groups.

Index

Index